"Emotional word pictures can enrich your every conversation and relationship. They will enable your words to penetrate the heart of your listener —to the extent that your listener will truly understand and even *feel* the impact of what you say. Word pictures form a language of love everybody can speak."

—Gary Smalley and John Trent

GARY SMALLEY, president of Today's Family in Phoenix, holds a bachelor's degree in psychology and has a master of divinity degree from Bethel Seminary in St. Paul, Minnesota. His previous bestselling books include *If Only He Knew, For Better or for Best* and *The Key to Your Child's Heart.* He and John Trent team-teach the *Love Is a Decision* seminar in cities across the United States and Canada. Gary and his wife, Norma, are the parents of three children: Kari, Greg and Michael.

JOHN TRENT, vice president of Today's Family, works in partnership with Gary Smalley. He has a Ph.D. in marriage and family counseling and holds a master's degree in New Testament Greek from Dallas Theological Seminary. He coauthored with Gary the bestselling books *The Blessing, The Gift of Honor, The Language of Love, Love Is a Decision, The Two Sides of Love* and *Home Remedies.* He lives in Phoenix with his wife, Cynthia, and their daughters, Kari Lorraine and Laura Katherine.

Books by Gary Smalley & John Trent, Ph.D.

The Blessing
The Gift of Honor
The Language of Love

Published by POCKET BOOKS

The
LANGUAGE
of
LOVE

. . . .

GARY SMALLEY &
JOHN TRENT, PH.D.

POCKET BOOKS

New York   London   Toronto   Sydney   Tokyo   Singapore

POCKET BOOKS, a division of Simon & Schuster Inc.
1230 Avenue of the Americas, New York, NY 10020

Copyright © 1988, 1991 by Gary Smalley and John Trent, Ph.D.

Published by arrangement with Focus on Family Publishing

ISBN 0-671-75047-X

First Pocket Books printing April 1992

10   9   8   7   6   5   4   3   2   1

POCKET and colophon are registered trademarks of
Simon & Schuster Inc.

Cover design by Darlene Barbaria

Printed in the U.S.A.

*To Norma and Cindy, two faithful and loving wives,
who are like our favorite gold-leaf novel.
Each day, with each new page of life,
we discover a fresh way to love
and be thankful for them.*

*And to Jim and Suzette Brawner,
world champions at using word pictures
to build a loving and lasting relationship.*

ACKNOWLEDGMENTS

We express our deepest thanks to the following people:

To Terry Brown, our faithful friend and ministry partner, for shouldering many extra hours of work while we were away writing this book.

To Steve Lyon, for his last-minute heroics; and to Penni Stewart, who also helped to bear the many extra burdens that came with creating this book.

To Lee and Susan Noble for providing a beautiful chalet where the original outline of this book came together.

To Doug Childress for his faithful friendship and wise words of critique and counsel

To Steve and Barbara Ulhman for their love, help, and support.

To Diana Trent, for her brilliant work in researching quotes and proofreading this manuscript.

To S. Rickly Christian, Rolf Zettersten, Mark Maddox, Janet Kobobel, Nancy Wallace, Teresa Wilson, Irene Goslaw, Diane Passno, and the rest of the

Acknowledgments

Focus on the Family team for their tremendous encouragement and support—especially Dr. James Dobson.

To Jim, Pam, Ryan, and Heather McGuire for their invaluable friendship and for providing an apple of great price.

And to Dorothy Shellenberger, Ann Kitchens, Tim Kimmel, Ken Gire, Tom Rietveld, Ted and Lynn Kitchens, Karen Cavan, Troy and Myra Hutchings and many other special friends who faithfully read the early versions of this manuscript and gave wise counsel, correction, and advice.

And to Larry Weeden, our much-valued editor.

AUTHORS' NOTE ON THE REVISED EDITON

Thank you for picking up *The Language of Love*. If this is your first time to read the book, you're about to discover the most powerful concept we've ever seen for adding life, power and depth to your words. If you read the first edition and are coming back to the book as a refresher or to share in a group, you'll find some important changes in this edition.

In a new chapter, you'll discover four ways in which emotional word pictures can deepen and strengthen your Christian walk. Word pictures can help to rekindle your prayer life, bring hope and encouragement to a hurting heart, and provide a powerful tool for evangelism.

Also, those of you who read the first edition will notice that we've changed some of the material in what is now chapter 4, "Unlocking the Gateway to Intimacy." When we first wrote this book, we wanted to support an observation we've made in working with thousands of couples and singles over the years. Namely, there are major, God-given differences in the ways the average man and woman communicate.

Men tend to share facts and speak a "language of the head." When the average man runs out of facts to talk about, he stops talking. However, most women have a strong natural ability and desire to share feelings, needs and hurts, a "language of the heart" that they long to have spoken in their homes.

In the first edition, we referred to right- and left-brain research as seeming to support those natural communication differences. All such references, however, have now been removed. Since the book came out, we have talked with several friends who have researched this area closely, and they have helped us to see that the validity of such research is not clear-cut. In addition, such research has been linked to negative psychological assumptions that we did not then—nor do we now—intend to support.

We sincerely apologize if we offended anyone by quoting such research. Our prayer is that the important message of this book will be judged by its scriptural support, for it was in the Bible's extensive use of word pictures that we first came to see this powerful communication tool. From Scripture's unshakable base we wrote this book and now offer you this expanded edition.

CONTENTS

Contents

**How can word pictures help my marriage
and family life?**

**How can word pictures help my walk
with God?**

Can word pictures be misused?

**A treasury of word pictures
at your fingertips**

WHAT IS A
WORD
PICTURE?

CHAPTER ONE

When Everyday Words Are Not Enough

Judy sat at the kitchen table, feeling more lonely and discouraged than at any other time in her life. Only a few hours earlier, she had come face to face with her worst fears. Now, try as she might, she couldn't stop wishing she could turn back the clock and undo what had happened. Slumped in her chair, she blinked back the tears and kept replaying the scene over and over in her mind . . .

It was early afternoon on a cool, fall day. Judy drove her new Buick past the rows of well-kept houses. Each was a monument to someone's climb up the ladder of success.

Judy fit perfectly into the upper-class neighborhood. Her blond hair and fair complexion were a tribute to her Swedish ancestry. And at thirty-nine, she still looked as young and trim as many of her friends in their late twenties. Her striking blue eyes flashed with satisfaction as she pulled into the driveway of her two-story, Victorian home. Columns of red brick laced with ivy, together with the manicured

3

lawn, reflected just the right blend of formality and warmth. Her two children were off at school, so the house would be quiet. After a full morning of shopping and errands, she looked forward to a few moments to unwind.

Pulling into the garage, Judy lingered in the car. Closing her eyes, she let the last strands of a haunting love song carry her away to a moonlit beach. Finally, with a sigh, she turned off the stereo, opened the car door, and began unloading the trophies of her morning's conquest. Carrying a sack of groceries in one hand and her keys in the other, she opened the garage entry door.

What Judy didn't realize was that she was also opening the door to the most painful discovery of her life.

Crossing the floor to the kitchen, she put the groceries down on the island counter. When she turned around, her eyes were caught by a sheet of notebook paper taped to the refrigerator.

She recognized the handwriting immediately. It was her husband's. On the outside of the folded piece of paper he'd written, "Judy, don't let the kids read this."

Don't let the kids read this? she thought to herself. *If they'd seen this before I did, they'd have read it in a second!*

As she unfolded the note, she tried to shrug off the uneasy feeling that suddenly came over her. She struggled to convince herself that the message would concern merely their business or personal finances. *That's why he didn't want the children to see what was inside,* she thought. But her hands trembled as she began to read:

Dear Judy,
  We both know we've been drifting apart for a

long time. And let's face it, I don't see you or anything between us changing one bit.

You may as well know that I've been seeing another woman. Yes, we've been involved, and I really think I love her. I'm telling you all this because somebody is bound to see us together, and I wanted to tell you before someone else did.

Judy, let's make this as easy as we can on the children. It doesn't have to be a big thing with the kids unless you want it to be.

I don't love you anymore, and I really wonder if I ever did. I've already had my attorney draw up the papers because I want a divorce—now.

I've got to go out of town on a business trip. I'll be back in two weeks and will come by to pick up some things and say hello to the kids. One more thing. I'll be staying at an apartment I've rented until this is over.

Steve

Judy clutched the note in her hand as her eyes flooded with tears. Her mind flashed back to a moment in childhood when a slip of paper tore away another important person from her life. She was five years old when the War Department sent the unwanted telegram—two paragraphs regretfully informing her family that her father was the latest casualty of the Korean War.

All these years later, a few paragraphs scratched on a sheet of paper loosed another avalanche of emotional pain. She had again lost the most important man in her life, but this time the note bore no hint of regret. Memories and hurtful emotions collided within Judy's mind, leaving her inviting, once-tranquil world in shambles. In response to her tears and heart-wrenching sobs, her beautiful home offered nothing but silence.

Judy was devastated. But she hadn't reached bottom yet. The worst was yet to come.

From Darkness to Despair

The family went fourteen days without hearing from Steve. During that time, Judy somehow managed to survive the chilling, devastating force of her emotions. Fully a hundred times a day, Steve's handwritten words crashed through her mind. And with each remembrance, she was left to pick up more pieces from her shattered heart.

I've been seeing another woman . . . Yes, we've been involved . . . I want a divorce . . . I'll be staying in my apartment until this is over . . .

Waiting for Steve to call or come by was a daily, emotional roller coaster. Each trip up the stairs, Judy passed walls lined with smiling family pictures. And each glance at them was a painful journey through nineteen years of marriage and the raising of two children.

Every opened drawer, every closet door left ajar, every corner of the house held its silent reminder of love lost. For almost half her life she had loved and shared herself with one man—someone who said he didn't care anymore, and may *never* have cared. But looking at her children's faces caused the most agony.

Night after night, in spite of her own inner hurt, Judy had to be both comforter and counselor to her son and daughter. She tried her best to put up a good front and explain what had happened. But how could she answer a seven-year-old boy's endless questions, especially when she didn't know the answers herself?

Mommy, why isn't Daddy coming home? Is he mad at me? Mommy, what have we done?

And how could she deal with her teenage daughter's angry fits that erupted every time her father's name was mentioned? In his note, Steve had written so offhandedly, "It doesn't have to be a big thing with the kids." But every tear Judy dried from her children's eyes ripped holes in his logic.

Each evening, after watching their sadness and confusion finally succumb to a fitful sleep, Judy would finally escape to her own bedroom. There, her mind crowded with lonely thoughts, she would cry herself to sleep in a queen-sized bed that suddenly seemed ten times too large.

As another evening crawled by, she wondered for the hundredth time, *Is there any chance we'll ever get back together?* No sooner had the thought drifted through her mind than the phone rang. It was Steve.

"Hello, Judy," he said in a detached, emotionless tone.

"Hello, Honey," she answered automatically, the words slipping out before she had time to think.

Honey? Why did I say that? she scolded herself. She wanted to be angry with him. She *was* angry with him. But now that he'd finally called, the anger she'd struggled with for days seemed to momentarily step aside.

Hearing Steve's voice made her yearn to see him again. She ached for him to put his arms around her . . . tell her that he still loved her . . . that it had all been just a terrible mistake.

But when Steve began to talk, all hope drained from her heart. His words came fast and cold.

"I'm glad you're home, Judy," he said. "I'm calling from the car phone and I'm on my way over to drop off some papers. I can't stop and talk now. We've tried talking for years, but it's never helped." His words carried the biting edge of a north wind in January. "I'll be there in a few minutes."

Before Judy could respond, the phone went dead in her hand. She shot up from her chair and hurried upstairs to tell the children their father was coming over. And as she went back downstairs and waited in the living room, thoughts cascaded down on her from nearly two decades of marriage.

They had always struggled to communicate with each other, even during their courtship. Over the years, arguments had accompanied far too many conversations. The fallout from their cold war of words had chilled their relationship and frozen a layer of insecurity deep within their children's lives.

For all Judy's married life, only one thing remained consistent. She had always longed for Steve to understand her feelings, needs, fears, goals, and wishes. *If only he could understand me; if only I could relate to him in a way he respected; if only we could both get beyond the arguments and angry words and communicate in-depth with each other; if only . . .*

Suddenly, the headlights of a car flashed through the living room window. Judy paused for a moment, quickly looked at herself in the hallway mirror, and straightened her skirt. Then she opened the front door and stepped out onto the porch. But as she stood watching Steve walk toward her, she noticed his car. The lights were still on; the engine was running.

Her eyes instantly opened wide, and she leaned forward, almost involuntarily. *Oh, no,* she gasped, blinking in disbelief. *He's brought the woman with him!*

The street light pushed back some of the darkness, and though Judy couldn't see clearly, there *was* a woman sitting in the front seat. Whoever it was, she refused to look up.

Steve walked up to the porch. He looked as handsome as ever, but his eyes lacked even a spark of warmth. "Here are some papers I want you to read," he said abruptly, thrusting a manila envelope at her.

"There's a legal document you need to sign and return to me as soon as possible."

"Steve!" Judy cried, pushing the folder back into his hands. "I can't sign any papers. I don't even know if I *want* to sign them. We need to talk with someone first. Can't we go to a counselor or a pastor or—"

"Now listen, Judy." Steve's voice rang in the cool night air. "I'm not putting things up for a vote. We've talked for years, and nothing's ever changed. I've thought this through, and I'm not interested in hearing you say for the thousandth time, 'It'll work out.' Let's get this straight. It's *not* going to work out. This marriage is through. Over! Finished! I want out! It's time I got on with my life."

Suddenly, there was a sound behind them in the doorway.

"But what about *our* lives, Dad?"

Neither Steve nor Judy had heard their teenage daughter come down the stairs. She stepped to her mother's side. "Dad, I can't believe you're doing this! What are you trying to prove? We love you so much, and this is so embarrassing."

"Kimberly, you just don't understand," her father began, extending his arms toward her.

"Don't touch me! Don't ever touch me again!" Kimberly sobbed as she pushed him away. "I can't believe you're doing this to Mom and me. And what about Brian? You don't care about him, either, do you?" Her tear-stained face was a mixture of anger and terrible sadness.

"I do care. But I'm not going to stand here and argue like this. Anybody could drive by and see us. Your mother and I . . . well, we just can't talk anymore. We've *never* been able to talk. I can't explain it, but we just don't get through to each other."

"But Dad—"

"Look!" he said, his voice blasting like a rifle shot. "I'm not going to get into this now! I've got to go; the car's running. I'll try to drop by or call or something later this week."

He turned abruptly and stormed off the porch. But then just as suddenly, he turned back and said, "Say hello to Brian for me." With that, he walked back to the car—and out of their lives.

Kimberly ran up the stairs to her room, crying. Judy stood frozen at the front door, watching her husband and another woman drive away. As the red taillights shimmered through her tears and disappeared into the darkness, she kept asking herself, *Why did this have to happen? Why? Why? Why?*

The Language of Love: Moving Beyond Everyday Words

Judy and Steve faced an all-too-common problem that was ripping apart their marriage: failure to communicate in a meaningful way. It's not that they hadn't tried to talk. Over the years they had spoken thousands of words to each other. But their lack of communication skills kept their marriage in shallow waters. They were never able to attain the depths of love and compassion for which they both longed. As with many other couples, their relationship wasn't ruined because of a lack of words. Their problem was that everyday words were not enough to provide insight, intimacy, and understanding.

If we're serious about having meaningful, fulfilling, productive relationships, we can't afford to let inadequate communication skills carry our conversations.

Our need to communicate with another person may not be as dramatic as Judy's was that night. But for all of us, our communication skills directly relate to how successful we'll be in our marriages, families, friendships, and professions. And if we're serious about having meaningful, fulfilling, productive relationships, we can't afford to let inadequate communication skills carry our conversations. There's got to be a *better* way of connecting with others in our lives—a way that can guide us safely into the depths of love.

You may be a parent getting nowhere trying to talk with your teenager; a married person in a growing or struggling relationship; a friend groping for the right words to encourage an emotionally hurt neighbor; a boss who can't seem to motivate or explain an important concept to your employee; a worker trying to express an important point to your supervisor; a teacher struggling to get a class to listen and remember what is taught; a counselor attempting to maneuver behind a couple's defenses and bring change to their relationship; a minister or public speaker who wants to challenge and stir people to action; a politician trying to sway the thoughts of a state or nation; or even a writer trying to capture a reader's heart.

No matter who you are or what you do, you can't escape the need to communicate meaningfully with others. And without exception, we all will run into the limitation of everyday expressions.

In a world awash with words, can we find a way to add new depth to what we say? Can a wife find a method to penetrate her husband's natural defenses and get her point across so he will long remember it? Can a man express himself more vividly or say the same old thing in a brand-new way? Can men and women say more by using fewer words?

To all the above, the answer is a resounding *YES!* Largely unused in marriages, homes, friendships, and businesses is a tool that can supercharge communication and change lives. This concept is as old as ancient kings but is so timeless that it has been used throughout the ages in every society. It's a powerful communication method we call *emotional word pictures.*[1]

Unlike anything else we've seen, this concept has the capacity to capture a person's attention by simultaneously engaging a person's thoughts and feelings. And along with its ability to move us to deeper levels of intimacy, it has the staying power to make a lasting impression of what we say and write. With fewer words, we can clarify and *intensify* what we want to communicate. In addition, it enables us to open the door to needed changes in a relationship.

This method can challenge the most intellectual adult, yet can be mastered by a child. In fact, we were astonished at how Kimberly, the teen in our opening story, quickly learned and dramatically applied an emotional word picture when faced with the breakup of her parents' marriage.

Journey with us for the next several chapters as we discover the primary method that:

- ancient wise men used to penetrate the hearts and minds of men and women;
- Abraham Lincoln and Winston Churchill utilized to inspire their countries in times of great peril;
- Hitler used to capture and twist the soul of a nation;
- professional counselors employ to speed up the healing process in broken relationships;
- coaches and trainers use to inspire and motivate professional athletes;
- top sales managers utilize to train effective employees; and

- comics and cartoonists have mastered to make us laugh while challenging us to think.

And, most importantly, emotional word pictures *can enrich your every conversation and relationship*. That is, they will enable your words to penetrate the heart of your listener—to the extent that your listener will truly understand and even *feel* the impact of what you say.

Word pictures form a language of love everybody can speak. Specifically, it was this language of love that confronted the barriers surrounding Judy's husband. In the next chapter we'll examine the amazing results of how this irresistible means of communication met the immovable heart of a runaway father.

CHAPTER TWO

Words That Penetrate
the Heart

During the three weeks following the tearful scene on the front porch, Steve called a few times. He even came by the house twice—once to pick up his mail, the other to gather more of his clothes and personal belongings.

Whenever he called or visited the house, he would talk for a few minutes with Judy or the children. But his conversations were never more than skin deep. After skillfully dodging all meaningful questions, he would finally invent some excuse to end the conversation and get on to his next "important" commitment.

Not being home at night, Steve never witnessed the aftermath of his leaving. He never saw the confusion that grew into continual heartache for Brian or how his young son's schoolwork and self-confidence were affected. Steve didn't recognize the seething emotions directed toward him by his daughter, Kimberly, and how that anger flared at every person she had ever trusted.[1]

Nor did he watch his wife valiantly struggle to

control her emotions in front of the children, only to retire at night and erupt with alternating fits of rage and brokenness. After crying herself to sleep, she would roll over in the middle of the night to snuggle next to him, only to awaken with her arms holding a pillow.

Judy, who hurt so badly herself, witnessed her son and daughter struggle through painful emotions. As she watched them suffer, not knowing quite how to help, a scene from her own childhood flashed back to her mind.

There had been a terrible rainstorm one summer day. She could see herself standing at the window, looking out on the backyard. As she watched, the wind and rain furiously lashed at the trees. After the storm, she walked into the yard and saw a nest of baby birds that had been blown to the ground. The emotions she felt for those tiny creatures crying out, floundering in the mud, and looking so helpless, frightened, and confused, were the same emotions she now felt as she watched her own children.

That's when she decided to seek counseling. Steve was adamant that he would never step into a counselor's office. Yet Judy felt she and the kids should go, if only for their sake. It was during those sessions that Kimberly learned about word pictures—and her first attempt to craft one broke through to her father's heart.

A Daughter's Life-Changing Words

More than two months after Steve's decision to leave the family, his stubborn heart met its match.

After a long, hectic day at work, Steve slowly scaled the two flights of stairs to the empty apartment that had once looked like freedom. He tossed aside yesterday's paper that was draped across an overstuffed chair, then flopped down to catch his breath.

Pulling out his briefcase, he began thumbing through various envelopes. He usually read his mail at the office. However, because the day had been so demanding, this was his first chance to leaf through the stack of letters that begged to be read. He found the usual collection of brochures and bills, along with a few interesting-looking business letters proudly sporting their embossed corporate logos.

But as he glanced at the pile before him, his eyes caught sight of a personal letter—one with handwriting that looked like his wife's. Looking closer, he saw it was actually from his daughter.

Through the years, Steve probably had been closer to Kimberly than to either his wife or his son. He'd always been frustrated by his wife's "unrealistic" expectations that he spend more time with his family than at work. And even at seven years old, Brian was already too much like Steve. Seeing his son was like looking in the mirror, and Steve was uncomfortable with the reflection. But it was different with Kimberly. When he talked to her, he didn't hear an echo of his own unhappiness. Her self-confidence and independence were traits he could respect.

Steve opened the letter, expecting to find a card or note. But what he found was far different. Inside was an emotional word picture his daughter had written—a story that would sink into his mind and heart, and hang on like the talons of a full-grown eagle:

Dear Daddy,

It's late at night, and I'm sitting in the middle of my bed writing to you. I've wanted to talk with you so many times during the past few weeks. But there never seems to be any time when we're alone.

Dad, I realize you're dating someone else. And I know you and Mom may never get back together. That's terribly hard to accept—especially knowing that you may never come back home or be an "everyday" dad to me and Brian again. But at least I want you to understand what's going on in our lives.

Don't think that Mom asked me to write this. She didn't. She doesn't know I'm writing, and neither does Brian. I just want to share with you what I've been thinking.

Dad, I feel like our family has been riding in a nice car for a long time. You know, the kind you always like to have as a company car. It's the kind that has every extra inside and not a scratch on the outside.

But over the years, the car has developed some problems. It's smoking a lot, the wheels wobble, and the seat covers are ripped. The car's been really hard to drive or ride in because of all the shaking and squeaking. But it's still a great automobile—or at least it could be. With a little work, I know it could run for years.

Since we got the car, Brian and I have been in the backseat while you and Mom have been up front. We feel really secure with you driving and Mom beside you. But last month, Mom was at the wheel.

It was nighttime, and we had just turned the corner near our house. Suddenly, we all looked up and saw another car, out of control, heading straight for us. Mom tried to swerve out of the way, but the other car still smashed into us. The impact sent us flying off the road and crashing into a lamppost.

The thing is, Dad, just before being hit, we could see that you were driving the other car. And we saw something else: Sitting next to you was another woman.

It was such a terrible accident that we were all

rushed to the emergency ward. But when we asked where you were, no one knew. We're still not really sure where you are or if you were hurt or if you need help.

Mom was really hurt. She was thrown into the steering wheel and broke several ribs. One of them punctured her lungs and almost pierced her heart.

When the car wrecked, the back door smashed into Brian. He was covered with cuts from the broken glass, and he shattered his arm, which is now in a cast. But that's not the worst. He's still in so much pain and shock that he doesn't want to talk or play with anyone.

As for me, I was thrown from the car. I was stuck out in the cold for a long time with my right leg broken. As I lay there, I couldn't move and didn't know what was wrong with Mom and Brian. I was hurting so much myself that I couldn't help them.

There have been times since that night when I wondered if any of us would make it. Even though we're getting a little better, we're all still in the hospital. The doctors say I'll need a lot of therapy on my leg, and I know they can help me get better. But I wish it was you who was helping me, instead of them.

The pain is so bad, but what's even worse is that we all miss you so much. Every day we wait to see if you're going to visit us in the hospital, and every day you don't come. I know it's over. But my heart would explode with joy if somehow I could look up and see you walk into my room.

At night when the hospital is really quiet, they push Brian and me into Mom's room, and we all talk about you. We talk about how much we loved driving with you and how we wish you were with us now.

Are you all right? Are you hurting from the wreck? Do you need us like we need you? If you need me, I'm here and I love you.

Your daughter,
Kimberly

A week after sending her father the letter, Kimberly stayed home with Brian and her mother rather than attend an evening high-school football game. Actually, the choice was easy. Nursing a broken heart, she just didn't feel like cheering and laughing with friends. For several hours she sat in her room watching television, trying to get involved in an old movie. Finally, she gave up hiding from her loneliness and went downstairs to rustle up a snack. She wasn't really hungry, but she thought a full stomach somehow would help to fill her empty heart.

She put her hand on the railing and slowly descended the stairs. But halfway down, something caught her attention, and she looked up. Standing in the doorway was her father. She hadn't heard the doorbell and had no idea how long he'd been there.

Heartbeats were measured in hours as their eyes met. Kimberly felt that if she looked away, he would disappear.

"Daddy?" she finally said in a faltering voice, her heart leaping.

"Kimberly," her father answered. Then, with emotion filling his voice, he asked, "How's your leg, Honey?"

"My leg?"

"I got your letter."

"Oh . . . well, it hasn't been doing too well."

"I'm sorry I hurt you so badly, Kimberly. You don't

know how sorry I am," he said, fighting to control his voice. "Your letter came when I didn't know if I could ever return to the family. I felt I'd already gone too far from all of you ever to come back and try again. But your story showed me how much pain I'd caused you all. And to be honest, it made me face the fact that I'd been pretty banged up myself."

He looked at Kimberly and swallowed hard before continuing. "Is your mom upstairs? I'm not promising anything, but I think we need to get some counseling. There's a lot we have to work out."

It was Steve's handwritten note that had launched his entire family into deep, threatening waters. It was a second one—conveying an emotional word picture —that helped calm the waters and start their relationship back toward solid ground. While a word picture may not always carry such a dramatic and immediate impact, it can and did in this case. The result: Two days after Steve came home, he walked into our office for counseling with his wife. And not long afterward, he moved home for good.

What prompted such change in this man? In tears, his wife and daughter had pleaded with him to come back to the family. Yet their pleas hadn't touched him. It was an emotional word picture that finally penetrated his brick-walled heart and pried open his life to much-needed change.

Much More Than a Story

How could sharing a single story bring so much change to someone's life? Kimberly didn't understand how or why a word picture worked with her father; she was just thankful it did. As you'll soon discover, there are five powerful forces at work each time they're used.

In the following pages, we'll explore how and why this language of love is so effective. But first, let's briefly define this communication tool.

A concise definition would read something like this: An emotional word picture is a communication tool that uses a story or object to activate simultaneously the *emotions* and *intellect* of a person. In so doing, it causes the person to *experience* our words, not just hear them.

An emotional word picture is a communication tool that uses a story or object to activate simultaneously the *emotions* and *intellect* of a person. In so doing, it causes the person to *experience* our words, not just hear them.

In short, this communication skill brings to life the thoughts we want to express. By looking through the pages of history and at current communication research, we find that the evidence is clear: Whenever we need to communicate important information with another person, word pictures can multiply the impact of our message.[2]

With this definition in mind, let's put word pictures under the microscope and turn it up to full power. By doing so, we'll see how many couples have moved to a deeper level of intimacy and understanding in a single hour than they have in months of everyday conversations.

HOW CAN
WORD PICTURES
ENRICH MY COMMUNICATION?

CHAPTER THREE

Igniting the Power of Words

We've already seen how a word picture dramatically changed one man's heart. But that's nothing compared to seeing this same power change men throughout an entire nation!

Altering a man's actions or attitudes has always been difficult, and many women feel their husbands wear armor plating that deflects everything they say. But in 1942, Walt Disney demonstrated that the effective use of a movie-length word picture could blast through such barriers. In his popular movie *Bambi*, he painted a picture that went straight to their hearts. And almost overnight he took thousands of men's fingers off the trigger, nearly bankrupting the deer-hunting industry in the process.

The year before the animated film was released, deer hunting in the United States was a $9.5 million business. But when one particularly touching scene was shown—that of a yearling who sees his mother gunned down by a hunter—there was a dramatic change in many men's attitudes. The following season, deer hunters spent only $4.1 million on tags, permits, and hunting trips![1]

It's often been said that one picture is worth a thousand words, and that certainly proved true with *Bambi*. But what does this mean to a man or woman who has a deep need to express important feelings, concerns, or information with another? It's high time to trade in a thousand everyday words for one effective word picture.

There are definite reasons this communication method has such a dramatic impact on people. In this chapter, we'll explore five of them, providing the mortar to bond for a lifetime with those you care about.

Five Reasons Word Pictures Work So Effectively

1. Word Pictures Have Been Time-Tested by the World's Greatest Communicators.

Your destiny may not lie in making front-page news. But if you want to leave a lasting impression on your own page of history, you'll do well to follow the lead of the world's greatest communicators.

Take Cicero, the silver-tongued orator of the Roman Empire. He believed word pictures are "lights" that illuminate truth. As he told his students, "The more crucial the message, the brighter the lights must be."[2]

In fact, he reported that a man was considered wise only if he could fit his thoughts within the frame of a word picture.[3]

Aristotle, one of the most respected scholars of early Greece, was a master at doing that very thing. For example, he once said of a fallen hero:

He entered the combat in body like the strongest bull, in spirit like the fiercest lion. Proving the old adage true, "A soldier is to come back from battle with his shield . . . or on it."[4]

Centuries later, Benjamin Franklin challenged the heart of his young country by crafting his thoughts with this same communication technique. Word pictures filled his speeches and writings, but perhaps the best example of his skill at using them is the epitaph he wrote for his own tombstone:

The body of Benjamin Franklin, Printer (like the cover of an old book, its contents torn out and stripped of its lettering and gilding), lies here, food for worms; but the work shall not be lost, for it will (as he believed) appear once more in a new and more elegant edition, revised and corrected by the Author.[5]

Prior to the Civil War, Harriet Beecher Stowe was enraged at the system of slavery down South. But who would listen to her? During the early years of American history, there was no platform from which a woman could speak. Yet an entire nation was greatly moved when she penned a book-length word picture called *Uncle Tom's Cabin*.

When her book was released, it inflamed those in the North. Her vivid description of the cruelest of slave owners fanned widespread opposition. Her message caused such white-hot fury that Abraham Lincoln felt the Civil War was inevitable.[6]

Nearly a century later, as a world war raged throughout Europe, another great communicator stepped forward. Winston Churchill always carried a look of utter defiance. It showed itself in the cigar shoved to one corner of his mouth and the warrior's glint in his eyes. But for a nation under siege, it was

Churchill's picture-filled speeches that rallied the fighting spirit of his shaken countrymen.

Soon after the humiliating retreat at Dunkirk, Britain faced the discouraging news that Italy had joined ranks with the Nazis. But in typical style, Churchill went on the radio with these words:

> Mussolini is a whipped jackal, who, to save his own skin, has made of Italy a vassal state of Hitler's Empire. Today, he is frisking up by the side of the German tiger with yelps not only of appetite—that could be understood—but even of triumph. . . . It shall do him no good. Dictators may walk to and fro among tigers, but they dare not be deceived. The tigers are getting hungry too.[7]

If Churchill was a master of motivating his countrymen, across the English Channel was his evil equal, Adolf Hitler. As we'll see in a later chapter, he held the soul of a nation captive with his gripping word pictures.[8] We'll also illustrate the tragic way some people still twist the language of love into a language of hate. In so doing, they use something intended for good to manipulate, intimidate, control, and destroy others.

Word pictures need not be lengthy to deliver a tremendous punch. Some of the great communicators in recent years have used this technique to spice up a single thought in a speech. In his 1961 inaugural address, John F. Kennedy spoke of the need to "let every other power know that this hemisphere intends to remain the master of its own house."[9]

Also, Martin Luther King, Jr., challenged a segregated society:

Let us not seek to satisfy our thirst for freedom by drinking from the cup of bitterness and hatred.[10]

And Ronald Reagan, called by many "The Great Communicator," salted his conversations with story after story and analogies, such as "Let's win one for the Gipper!"[11]

A look across the pages of history confirms that word pictures have rocked the world. Perhaps nowhere is that more evident than in one treasured book.

Without question, the Bible has had the most life-changing effect of anything ever written. It remains the most widely read, circulated, and translated book in history.[12] Of all the communication methods the biblical writers could have used, word pictures surface on nearly every page.

Consider, for example, one of the Bible's most familiar passages, the oft-quoted Psalm 23, which begins, "The Lord is my shepherd . . ." This psalm has provided hope for people everywhere as they crossed through their own personal "valley of the shadow of death."

It was spoken on the bridge of the Titanic as lifeboats moved away from the doomed vessel,[13] on a beach at Okinawa and in the jungles of Vietnam in the midst of fighting,[14] in a space capsule orbiting the moon,[15] and is still spoken every day in hospital waiting rooms where families pray.

What astonished us in our research was finding that throughout the Scriptures, Jesus' primary method to teach, challenge, and motivate others was word pictures. When discussing love, He launched into a word picture about a good samaritan. To encourage His disciples, Jesus told them that in His Father's home, there were many mansions waiting for them. When teaching lessons of faith, He spoke of faith the size of a mustard seed moving a mountain. And to describe the forgiving heart of a father, He shared a story about a prodigal son.[16]

We'll go into much more detail in chapter 15, but word pictures are also the most frequent biblical means of describing who Jesus is. For example, He is pictured as the Wonderful Counselor, Everlasting Father, Prince of Peace, the Word, the Light of the World, the Vine, the Lion of the tribe of Judah, and the bright Morning Star.[17]

We've looked at men and women who have conveyed their most important messages with this language of love. By standing in the shadow of these giants, you can gain their advantage—the power to change and enrich lives. But this isn't the only reason for using word pictures. There are four more that can provide a bedrock foundation for building lasting relationships with others.

2. Word Pictures Grab and Direct Attention.

A wise husband or wife can uncover the secret that advertisers have used for years to capture a person's attention. Advertisers know they have only a few seconds to make their pitch. By wrapping brief word pictures around their corporate slogans, they ensure their message outlives their commercial. Who can forget slogans such as: "You're in good hands," "Own a piece of the rock," and "Like a good neighbor"? Similarly, we don't drive cars; we drive Broncos, Blazers, Colts, Cavaliers, and Mustangs.

Studies show that when we hear a word picture, our brain works faster and expends much more energy than while reading or listening to conventional words.[18] To illustrate, read a page of your favorite novel and an equal amount from the encyclopedia. You'll find yourself reading the novel much faster, and for good reason.

Your response to a story is like driving into a layer of fog along the California coast. You're instantly alert, working hard to spot what's ahead. You strain to see the divider lines, and your eyes ache as they search for brake lights. Your mind won't let you relax until you emerge from the fog and can see clearly again.

In like manner, an emotional word picture creates a mist in your listener's mind. It forces him to strain mentally to see what lies beyond your story. And when the fog lifts, the person finally breaks out into a more clear understanding of what you wanted to express. For a weekly example of this, just watch the sleepy heads snap up in the pews when a minister uses a well-timed illustration in the middle of a sermon!

Great communicators know that a word picture can give them an advantage from the moment they begin to speak.

It has been said that the first thirty seconds of a conversation are crucial.[19] Great communicators know that a word picture can give them an advantage from the moment they begin to speak. You can use this attention-grabbing advantage in your communication—even with hard-to-reach people.

That's what Kimberly found when she wrote to her father, a man who steered clear of confrontation. Her word picture held his attention fast—until the mist lifted, and he understood what she wanted to say.

3. Word Pictures Bring Communication to Life.

Another major reason for using word pictures is that they activate a person's emotions, which can lead to positive change. Up until the onset of puberty, children experience change primarily through straightforward teaching and instruction.[20] But once puberty hits, words alone have far less impact on a child. For adolescents and adults, life changes occur mainly through significant emotional events, such as a death, marriage, birth, loss of a parent, breaking off a relationship, winning or failing to win an award, or making a religious commitment.[21]

Word pictures simultaneously tap into a person's emotions, intellect, and will by creating a "theater of the mind" or "mental journey." As we read earlier, hunters who saw Disney's movie got more than they paid for. Many of them emotionally experienced the dark side of their sport for the first time. Instead of reveling in the thrill of the hunt, they felt the emotions of a youngster seeing its mother gunned down.

Studies have shown that word pictures not only activate our emotions, but they also *physically* affect us.[22] That is, when we hear a story about either a real or imaginary event, our five senses are triggered almost as if we experienced the event ourselves![23]

That helps explain why you can feel so drained after reading a thrilling book or why a suspenseful movie wears you out. In reality, you're safely curled up in your chair, far removed from the crazed tribe of cannibals. But physiologically you experience the same shortness of breath and the release of chemicals that pour into the hero's bloodstream.[24]

Not only does fear prompt this reaction, but so do love and other positive emotions. Many women are in marriages devoid of emotional warmth. Where do they turn for romance millions of times a year? To the picture of love painted in romantic novels. Reading about someone else's romance (real or imagined) causes these women to experience, at least in some measure, the longed-for feelings of love.

When Kimberly mailed her word picture to her

father, she actually sent him a time bomb. Her words exploded inside him, forcing him to experience physically and emotionally the damage he had caused others. And, as mentioned earlier, awakened emotions can prompt changes in one's thinking. What's more, we plant within a listener a lasting seed that can grow into a changed life—even if that person rejects our words at first hearing.

4. Word Pictures Lock Thoughts into Our Memory.

We typically hear one or both parties in a struggling marriage complain, "Why can't he (or she) remember what I say?" Actually, frustrated spouses aren't the only ones who feel they're talking to deaf ears and forgetful minds.[25]

A constant complaint of ministers, teachers, and other educators is that people don't remember what they've been taught. In part, this is because so much teaching is done by straight lecture. There are certain advantages to this mode of instruction. However, after a few hours, the average person will remember only 7 percent of a half-hour speech!

As you might suspect, researchers have shown that people remember concepts and conversations far longer and much more vividly when a word picture is used. In fact, the more novel or bizarre the story or object, the longer the concept is remembered!

Corrie ten Boom, a Holocaust survivor and noted worldwide speaker, impressed this principle on us. "Don't ever step in front of a group without an object or story that illustrates what you're saying," she would tell us in her firm, heavily accented voice. "Every place I speak, I use one. And even when I've been away for years, people still remember what I've said."

In her travels, Corrie became a symbol of hope to anyone in spiritual or physical bondage. When she spoke before a group, she often held up a large piece of embroidery with the back side showing. Strings hung every which way, and no clear pattern could be discerned.

"This is the way our lives often look," she would say. "When I was in the concentration camp, it seemed there was nothing but ugliness and chaos. But then I looked to God to make sense of my world"—at that point she would turn the tapestry around, revealing to her audience a beautifully embroidered crown —"and at last I could see why He added a certain thread or color, no matter how painful the stitching."

Like the memory of a moon-lit walk, word pictures linger long after they've been spoken. When Kimberly sent her letter to her father, it made an immediate impact on his life. However, he told us later that it was its lasting impact—the way it stayed in his mind for days and continued to convict him—that broke through to his heart.

5. Word Pictures Provide a Gateway to Intimacy.

As powerful as these four reasons are to use emotional word pictures, they're overshadowed by the fifth: Word pictures open the door to very meaningful and intimate relationships.

In nearly every home, major problems can surface because men and women have markedly different ways of thinking and talking. But emotional word pictures help couples find common ground for communication.

Time and again we've seen dull, unfulfilling marriages transformed into vibrant, mutually satisfying relationships. It doesn't happen by magic or without consistent work. It happens because people discover the gateway to intimacy through the language of love. And we'll show you how in the next chapter.

CHAPTER FOUR

Unlocking the Gateway to Intimacy

A number of years ago, I (Gary) sat down to talk with an attractive woman who was in obvious pain. With tears streaming down her face, she sobbed, "I've tried to express what's wrong in our marriage, but I just can't seem to explain it. What's the use in bringing it all up again?"

After only five years of marriage, this woman had nearly given up hope of experiencing a loving, healthy, and lasting relationship with her husband. Opposed to divorce, she had resigned herself to a life that offered few of the wishes and dreams she once longed for.

I had heard this kind of story before. For years, I had regularly counseled with husbands and wives, spending countless hours talking to them about improving their relationships. Only now, I wasn't sitting in my counseling office. I was seated at my kitchen table. And the woman sitting across from me wasn't a counselee—she was my own wife, Norma!

That day, I made a decision to understand what was happening, or not happening, in my marriage. And I also decided to find the answers to several important questions. Why was Norma feeling so frustrated in her attempts to communicate with me? Why did I have such a difficult time sharing my feelings with her? And why was it such a struggle to understand each other—particularly when we discussed important issues?

It isn't until we understand some of the ways God has equipped men and women differently that we will begin to maximize our communication.

It wasn't until we understood some of the ways God has equipped men and women differently that we began maximizing our communication. The bridge that spanned these differences proved to be word pictures.

Have you ever tried to express an important thought or feeling with members of the opposite sex, only to have them act as if you're speaking a foreign language? Have you ever asked, "Why can't he (or she) *feel* what I'm saying?" Join the club.

Throughout history, many women have found it difficult (some say impossible!) to communicate with men. And an equal number of men have given up trying to converse with women. I ran into this problem myself on a shopping trip when my wife and I were using the same words, but speaking a different language.

"Shoooooppping"

After that tearful session with my wife, I decided to commit myself wholeheartedly to understanding and relating to her. But I didn't know where to start.

Suddenly, I had an idea that I knew would get me nominated for Husband of the Year. I could do something adventurous with Norma—like going shopping! Of course! My wife loves to shop. Since I had never volunteered to go with her before, this would demonstrate how much I really cared. I could arrange for a baby-sitter and then take her to one of her favorite places in the world: the mall!

I'm not sure what emotional and physiological changes ignite inside my wife upon hearing the words "the mall," but when I told her my idea, it was obvious something dramatic was happening. Her eyes lit up like a Christmas tree, and she trembled with excitement—the same reaction I'd had when someone gave me two tickets to an NFL play-off game.

That next Saturday afternoon, when Norma and I went shopping together, I ran face first into a major barrier that bars many men and women from meaningful communication. What I discovered blew open the door to understanding and relating to Norma, and steered me toward emotional word pictures for help. Here's what happened:

As we drove up to the mall, Norma told me she needed to look for a new blouse. So after we parked the car and walked into the nearest clothing store, she held up a blouse and asked, "What do you think?"

"Great," I said. "Let's get it." But really, I was thinking, *Great! If she hurries up and gets this blouse, we'll be back home in plenty of time to watch the college game on TV.*

Then she picked up another blouse and said, "What do you think about this one?"

"It's great, too!" I said. "Get either one. No, get both!"

But after looking at a number of blouses on the rack, we walked out of the store empty-handed. Then we went into another store, and she did the same thing. And then into another store. And another. And another!

As we went in and out of all the shops, I became increasingly anxious. The thought even struck me, *Not only will I miss the halftime highlights, but I'll also miss the entire game!*

After looking at what seemed like hundreds of blouses, I could tell I was beginning to lose it. At the rate we were going, I would miss the entire season! And that's when it happened.

Instead of picking up a blouse at the next store we entered, she held up a dress that was our daughter's size. "What do you think about this for Kari?" she asked.

Taxed beyond any mortal's limits, my willpower cracked, and I blurted out, "What do you mean, 'What do I think about a dress for Kari?' We're here shopping for blouses for you, not dresses for Kari!"

As if that wasn't bad enough, we left that store without buying anything, and then she asked if we could stop and have coffee! We'd already been at the mall for sixty-seven entire minutes, which beat my previous endurance record by *half an hour*. I couldn't *believe* it—she actually had the nerve to want to sit around and discuss the kids' lives!

That night, I began to understand a common difference between men and women. I wasn't shopping for blouses . . . I was *hunting* for blouses! I wanted to conquer the blouse, bag it, and then get back home where important things were, like my Saturday-afternoon football game!

My wife, however, looked at shopping from opposite extremes. For her, it meant more than simply buying a blouse. It was a way to spend time talking together as we enjoyed several hours away from the children—and Saturday afternoon football.

Like most men, I thought a trip to the mall meant

going shopping. But to my wife it meant *shoooooppping!*

Over the next several days, I thought back to our mall experience and my commitment to become a better communicator. As I reflected on our afternoon, I realized I had overlooked something important.

For years I had been confronted with unisex haircutters, unisex clothing, and coed dorms. Yet in the rush for equality of the sexes, I'd been lulled into overlooking an important aspect of healthy male/female relationships: recognizing and valuing the innate differences between men and women.

Of course, typical male/female differences don't apply to every relationship.[1] In some 15 percent of homes, the man may display more "typically" female tendencies when it comes to communication styles, and vice versa. This often occurs with men and women who are left-handed.[2] Yet male/female styles do predominate, even in homes where typical communication roles are reversed. In fact, virtually all relationships with role reversals experience as many differences as the most stereotypical couples.

With that in mind, let's examine several important ways men and women usually vary in the communication arena. We've witnessed many of them crop up around our house, and most likely you have, too. Interestingly, they're also the ones that physiologists have found to be common between the sexes.

The Little Buzzards Are Different, Aren't They?

In our home, we have our own version of the "Battle of the Sexes." On one side are Norma and our oldest child (and only daughter), Kari. The other consists of me, "the big kahuna," and our two sons, Greg and Michael.

Norma and I would testify before a live, televised

congressional hearing that we didn't brainwash our children into adopting typical male and female roles and reactions. But from the time they first showed signs of life, they displayed the common differences between the sexes. It all began with how much more *noise* came from the boys and how many more *words* came from our daughter at the same age.

Gaining the Edge in Communication

Researchers have found that from the earliest years little girls talk more than little boys.[3] One study showed that even in the hospital nursery, girls had more lip movement than boys![4] That propensity keeps right on increasing through the years, giving them an edge at meaningful communication!

In our home, Norma noticed the same thing discovered by Harvard's Preschool Program in its research of communication differences between the sexes.[5] After wiring a playground for sound, researchers studied all the noises coming from the mouths of several hundred preschool boys and girls.

The researchers found that 100 percent of the sounds coming from the girls' mouths were audible, recognizable words. The girls each spent a great deal of time talking to other children—and nearly as much talking to themselves!

As for the little boys, only 68 percent of their sounds were understandable words! The remaining 32 percent were either one-syllable sounds like "uh" and "mmm," or sound effects like "Varooom!" "Yaaaaah!" and "Zooooom!"

Norma was comforted to discover that the propensity males had in our family to yell and grunt was caused by genetics, not environment. And after twenty-plus years of asking me questions and receiving monosyllabic answers like "uh" and "mmm," she claims this inability to communicate in understandable sentences remains constant throughout the male lifespan!

Young men clearly have more difficulty communicating than young women. Special education teachers are aware of that, since nine out of ten speech pathology problems involve males.

But what about us adults? You'd certainly think grown men would have caught up with their wives when it comes to communication skills. But think again!

Studies show something that Norma and I have observed for years in our relationship. When it comes to the number of words each of us uses, her total count was quite a bit higher than mine. It's been found that the average man speaks roughly 12,500 words a day. In contrast, the average woman speaks more than 25,000![6]

In our marriage that meant when I got home from work, I'd already used my 12,500-word daily quota, while Norma was just getting warmed up! I was being paid to talk all day. I didn't want to come home and then talk all night! I wanted to park in front of the television set.

Not only did Norma leave me in the dust when it came to the number of words we spoke, but when we did talk, it seemed as if we were headed down two different roads. Let me illustrate what I mean.

For most men, "facts" are a major part of a conversation. For example, when Norma would meet me at the door, she'd often say, "Can we talk tonight?"

My first response was always, "About what?" Like Detective Joe Friday, most men want their wives to "Give me the facts, Ma'am, just the facts." Indeed, when the average male runs out of facts, he'll stop talking.

For years, Norma longed to discover my deepest feelings, especially when we faced an important issue or decision. But time and again, when the conversation moved beyond the nuts-and-bolts facts of the matter, I'd clam up or change the subject.

Like most women, Norma was far more in touch with her emotions than I was. I was good with giving her the bottom line, but the bottom of my feelings remained uncharted territory. The difference showed in our consistent failure to have meaningful conversations.

Two Languages in the Same Home

In many homes, the ways men and women communicate are so far apart that it's as if they're speaking two different languages—without an interpreter! What do we mean?

Over the past twenty years, we've interviewed several hundred couples and thousands of women all over the country. And we've found that most men speak what we call a "language of the head."

Call it "fact talk" or "head talk," it means the average man enjoys conquering five hundred highway miles a day on family vacations; favors mathematical formulas over Harlequin romances; remembers only the dictionary definition of love; and generally prefers clinical, black-and-white thinking. "Head talk" keeps most emotions bottled up, desiring instead to deal with the facts like memorized batting averages and box scores.

On the other hand, most women speak what we call a "language of the heart." They're comfortable with both facts *and* feelings.

Call it "heart talk" or "feeling talk," those who speak this language enjoy looking at the fine-detail work of quilts, are better able to use their imagination, and show a particular interest in deep relationships. They actually *like* to pull over at rest stops and read historical markers, and they usually don't care what's happening on a football field unless they personally know the players or their wives. They tend to express the feelings of love, not just the definition, and would rather read *People* magazine than *Popular Mechanics* because the former is more relational.

"There's a Stuckey's Up Ahead."

These mental differences were always painfully apparent when we (the Smalleys) took family vacations by car. I had spent hours plotting out the trip as if I were getting ready to drive the Indianapolis 500. I knew we had to be *on the road* each morning no later than 8 o'clock and make *exactly* 487 miles a day. And based on the 12.3 miles-per-gallon we got in our gas-guzzling tank, I even calculated where we'd stop for gas. I was determined to let nothing stand in my way. I would compromise only when absolutely necessary.

The first sign my goals were in jeopardy came when I felt Kari kicking the back of my seat.

"Cut that out," I'd say, my eyes glued to the bumper of a car I was trying to pass. I'd already passed about fifty that day, and I felt like John Wayne galloping toward the fort.

"I need to go to the bathroom."

"You'll have to wait," I replied, glancing first at the diminishing car in my rearview mirror, then at the odometer, then the dashboard clock, then the map. "We can stop in the next town."

"But Daddy!"

"Just another twenty-five miles."

Five minutes later, the boys alleged they were starving to death.

"I'm so hungry my stomach hurts," Mike, our youngest, would moan. "Oooohhhh! Oooowwww! Daddy, my stomach!"

"Mommy, it's past lunch time and Daddy won't stop!" Greg pitched in, seeking a higher authority.

"I can't wait any longer!" Kari shouted, kicking my seat.

"Quit kicking the seat," I replied. "Seventeen more miles."

Norma, looking at me as if I were a prison warden, pointed out a billboard as we sped down the interstate. And then ever so quietly and with a hint of a smile, she said, *"There's a Stuckey's up ahead."*

In our family, mentioning the word "Stuckey's" is the same as shouting, "Oasis ahead!" to people dying of thirst. My choice was made for me: I *had* to pull over at the next exit. My only consolation was that Stuckey's was a "three-star stop." That is, I could accomplish three tasks there at once: pit stop, gas stop, and food stop.

Practically before the car came to a stop, I jumped out to pump gas. Quickly, I shooed the kids toward the restroom and Norma toward the lunch counter.

"Please hurry!" I shouted, cringing as a line of cars whizzed by—cars I had passed just minutes before. "We've got to get back on the road and *catch* those cars!"

Differences, differences, differences! Why does it seem that God has given women such an advantage in personal communication and intimate relationships?

While some men look at a woman's communication

skills as a negative, they're actually one reason she's so valuable to him. In Genesis 2:18, we're told the woman was designed as a "helper" to complete the man. That word *helper*, in the language of the Old Testament, carries with it the idea of doing something for someone that he lacks the skill to do.

One kind of help the average woman brings to a man is the ability to share deep, meaningful communication.

Most men have the factual, logical "language of the head" down pat. They can come up with a lecture on the spot—but they're often *put* on the spot when they need to communicate words of warmth, love or encouragement.

If men are to be truly effective in their relationships both at home and at work, they need to develop the ability to speak the "language of the heart." And right there under the same roof are women who can help them learn those skills.

Wise husbands and wives will learn to speak each other's language, and they'll also teach their children to do so to help them enter marriage some day as effective communicators. Most boys do need training, as evidenced by the "backseat syndrome" that strikes the Smalley boys every vacation.

While on the road, listening to our daughter talk nonstop for an hour, Norma or I would always say, "Okay, Kari, it's time to let the boys speak. Boys, it's your turn to talk." After Kari quieted down, we were greeted by . . . silence. So Kari would start talking again.

Like the boys, I'm still playing catch-up to Norma and Kari in the quantity of words spoken. And there remain some "mysteries" when it comes to Norma and me understanding each other. But just because the females in our home have a natural communication advantage doesn't lead to frustration for us males anymore. If anything, we're taking lessons from them.

For men and women to communicate effectively, it takes both *knowledge* and *skills*. So far we have focused on the former—developing knowledge about the importance of communication and how innate male and female thinking patterns can short-circuit understanding. But what about the skills?

There is a way for a man to boost his communication skills instantly and for a woman to multiply hers. By using the power of emotional word pictures, a man can move beyond "facts" and begin to achieve total communication—feelings and facts—with a woman. This same skill not only will help a woman get a man to *feel* her words as well as *hear* them, but it also will maximize her God-given relational abilities.

Years ago, Norma proved this point to me. She illustrated a concern in such a way that her words immediately moved from my head to my heart.

Add Feelings to Facts.

When I was working on my parenting book, *The Key to Your Child's Heart,* I asked Norma if she would write one of the chapters. It was a section that highlighted one of her strengths, and I thought the project would be an easy and pleasurable experience for her. I thought wrong.

As the days passed and time drew near for the chapter to be completed, Norma hadn't even started. Several times she tried to discuss how much of a burden the project was, but I always steered the conversation back to the "facts."

I decided it was time to motivate her. I told her that writing a book was absolutely no big deal. She wrote excellent letters, I pointed out. She ought to think of the chapter as just one long letter to thousands of people she'd never met. What's more, I assured her that as a seasoned publishing veteran, I would personally critique each and every page and catch her slightest error. I thought to myself, *Is that motivation, or what?*

Her emotional, softhearted appeals to duck the assignment made little impact on me, because I was armed with the facts. But my logical, hardheaded reasoning didn't impress *her* much, either. We traded words as if we were swapping Monopoly money. Frankly, we should have saved our breath. We were at loggerheads until my wife, in desperation, gave me the following word picture.

"I know you don't realize it, Gary, but you're wearing me out emotionally and physically," she said.

"Who, me?"

"Come on, let's be serious for a minute. For the past several days you've been draining all my energy. I know you'll be upset by me bringing this up, but—"

"Me? Get upset?" I said, trying to keep things light. "If I'm draining your energy, tell me about it. It's no problem."

"Do you see those hills in the distance?" she asked, pointing out the window. "Every day I feel like I must climb them, wearing a twenty-pound backpack. Between getting the kids fed, dressed, to school, and to their athletic practices—and still managing our business office—I barely have enough energy to take another step.

"Now, don't get me wrong," she continued. "I work out to stay in shape, and I love walking those hills daily. But you're doing something that's like asking me to climb Squaw Peak every day—in addition to climbing those hills."

"I am?" I said, pondering her words. Several

months earlier I had climbed Squaw Peak, a beautiful mountain near our home, and I knew firsthand how demanding its incline was. My mind shifted into the hyper-search mode to determine where Norma was headed with the story. "Okay, I'm stumped," I finally said. "What in the world am I doing to force Squaw Peak on you?"

"You added Squaw Peak to my day when you asked me to write that chapter for the book. For you, carrying around a twenty-pound pack is nothing. But to me, the weight of my current responsibilities takes all my energy. Honey, I just can't add another pound, climb the hills, and take on Squaw Peak as well."

Suddenly, everything she had been saying before was clear. To me, writing a chapter wouldn't have added an extra ounce to my pack or caused the slightest additional incline to the hills I climb daily. But for the first time I could *feel* the strain I'd unknowingly put on her.

"If that's what writing this chapter is like, then I wouldn't want you to do it," I said without a moment's hesitation. "I appreciate what you're already doing and don't want to weigh you down any more. You're far too valuable for that."

After the conversation, it was as if a cloud lifted from our relationship. But I didn't know what to make of things the next morning when I came down the hall for breakfast. Norma was sitting at her kitchen desk, furiously writing away.

"What are you doing?" I asked, dumbfounded.

"Writing my chapter."

"You're doing *what?* I thought you said it was like climbing Squaw Peak!"

"It was," she said. "When I knew I had to write it, I felt tremendous pressure. But now that I don't *have* to, I feel like writing!"

Bridging the Communication Gap

Who said word pictures will help you understand *all* the differences between men and women? But they do help us bridge the natural communication gap— and better understand what another person is saying.

Let's go back to what happened when my wife first expressed her concerns about writing a chapter. Like a typical man, I focused on the facts—the actual words being said—to the exclusion of the emotions she was sharing. I failed to read between the lines. This isn't a fault peculiar to me. Something similar happened to a couple we know, and scenes like it probably take place in nearly every home.

It had been a particularly trying day for Diane, and everything that could go wrong around the house did go wrong. The moment her husband walked in the door that night, she nailed him. "Jack, you never help around the house," she complained. "I always have to take out the trash and do everything else. You *never* lift a finger to make my life any easier!"

After having his hair parted by her emotional words, Jack replied with a matter-of-fact voice. "Now, Diane. Are you sure I *never* help you? And do you *always* take out the trash? I took the garbage out just yesterday, and two days ago I mowed the lawn. And what about earlier this week when . . ."

What Jack didn't understand (and what can breed tremendous frustration between a husband and wife) is that Diane wasn't really talking about whether he took out the garbage. Rather, she was expressing her feelings about how she needed his support around the house. But like most males, Jack heard only his wife's literal words. The nonliteral, softhearted feelings behind her words zoomed right by him.

In addition to a woman's verbal skills, she has a built-in sensitivity that acts like a radar detector. It picks up the tone of voice used in a conversation, as well as the emotional or pictorial messages that are seen or spoken. If Diane had used a word picture to convey her message, she could have helped Jack *feel* what she was actually saying.

Remember, change occurs with adults when they *experience* an emotional event. When Norma first discussed not writing the chapter, her words only registered as black-and-white facts to me. Consequently, they had little effect. But when she used a word picture, it was as if she began talking in color instead. I immediately saw the colors and shades of her feelings, and as a result, both my attitudes and actions changed.

If a woman truly expects to have meaningful communication with her husband, she *must* reach his heart, not just his head. And if a man truly wants to communicate with his wife, he *must* enter her world of emotions. In both these regards, word pictures can serve as a tremendous aid. They won't eliminate all the differences between men and women, but they can enable us to unlock the gateway to intimacy.

Where Do You Go from Here?

If you haven't won any creative awards lately, you may be wondering how to paint effective word pictures. Where do you find them? When is the best time to use them in your most important relationships? In the coming pages, these questions will be answered. You'll learn the seven steps to creating word pictures, along with four ways to use them most effectively in everyday conversations.

Also, you'll be steered to four inexhaustible wells from which you can draw word pictures that work best in your specific situation, and you'll be shown how to apply them to make an immediate difference in your marriage and family life. If you're looking for even more ammunition to improve your communication, at the end of the book you'll find a treasury of more than one hundred word pictures, which you can use at home, in business, with friends, or in church.

Word pictures are the most powerful method of communication we know. Yet when it comes to this language of love, there are people who refuse to listen and aren't able to love back. In a later chapter, we'll talk about why some people remain resistant to any attempt at meaningful communication. We'll also see how these same people often harness the power of word pictures to hurt, manipulate, and control.[7] But thankfully, most people don't fall into this hard-to-reach category. Most men and women are open to change and intimacy, particularly when they're approached in a way that reaches straight to the heart.

Beginning in the next chapter, you'll start learning how to communicate with such power. And your relationships will never be the same.

HOW DO I CREATE A WORD PICTURE?

CHAPTER FIVE

Creating an Effective Emotional Word Picture

PART ONE

When it comes to cooking in the kitchen, most men act as if they are above reading instructions. I hate to admit it, but I (John) fall into that category. Basically, I feel that following a recipe is a sign of weakness.

In my few adventures in the kitchen, I've turned three-alarm chili into a twenty-three-alarm fireball, causing my wife, Cindy, and daughter, Kari Lorraine, to sprint to the sink and guzzle gallons of water. I've substituted cream of tartar for baking powder because "they looked the same to me!" I've even used peanut butter to "hold" a meat loaf together.

Despite my culinary creativity, most of my exploits have caused little damage other than heartburn and "panburn." But years ago, I nearly destroyed an entire apartment complex by ignoring a recipe.

It was Thanksgiving break, and my college roommates and I were spending the holiday in our apartment. Since we weren't going to be with our families, we invited a bunch of friends to join us for a home-cooked Thanksgiving feast.

As the day neared, we made up a shopping list, bought out the local grocery store, and began preparing for our sumptuous meal. From the beginning, I should have known we were in big trouble when my roommate couldn't figure out how to use the electric can opener. But the damage he inflicted on the can was a minor issue compared to what I did to the turkey.

Consider the facts. I knew I had an IQ of at least my age. (My wrestling coach told me that repeatedly.) At the very least, I knew I was more intelligent than the turkey I was supposed to cook. So why waste time reading directions on how to prepare it?

I had picked a mammoth bird that looked more like a small ostrich than a large turkey. As I removed the wrapper, I noticed a bag full of disgusting things shoved clear up inside the cavity. I debated whether or not to remove it, but I figured the butcher put it there for flavoring. So I left it in.

My next step was to "dress" the carcass. I had seen my mother rub peanut oil over turkeys to give them that golden-brown look. So, naturally, I planned to do the same with my masterpiece. The closest thing I could find was 3-in-1 oil, but I was smart enough not to use that. There wasn't enough left in the can, anyway. So I wrapped a sheet of aluminum foil around the bottom of the bird and proceeded to the oven, which I had remembered to preheat. In fact, I'd turned the thermostat to "torch" nearly an hour before to make sure it was hot enough.

My next in a long line of mistakes was to set "Turkey Kong" directly onto the metal rack in the oven. No baking pan. No cookie sheet. Nothing to catch the fat and grease. Just a paper-thin layer of foil separating an otherwise-naked, twenty-four-pound bird from the red-hot coils inches below.

While I'd already done enough to lead to disaster,

my most catastrophic error was deciding I had plenty of time to pick up a few friends who were coming to our holiday feast. I walked outside with a jaunty step, filled with pride that I could rescue two Thanksgiving orphans from cafeteria food. I nearly broke my arm patting myself on the back.

Making the leisurely, twenty-five-minute drive to their house without incident, I spent the return trip bragging to my captive audience about the great meal awaiting them. But rounding the corner for the final approach to our "banquet hall," I spotted the flashing red lights of several fire trucks at our apartment complex.

"Great!" I said. "A little drama! Let's go see what idiot burned down his apartment!"

As I soon discovered, the idiot was me. Black smoke was belching from the door of our apartment, which the firemen had smashed into toothpicks with axes. As if that wasn't embarrassing enough, they dragged out what was left of my charred, smoldering turkey and hosed it off on the grass!

Swallowing my pride, I drove my roommates and our invited guests to a local cafeteria for Thanksgiving dinner. And instead of eating turkey for leftovers, I ate crow for months.

That Thanksgiving was one of the most embarrassing moments of my life. But it illustrates an important point: We don't want your first attempt at using word pictures to go up in flames. We know that some of you are so excited to use this communication method that you're ready to "throw the turkey into the oven" without reading the instructions. But to avoid having to repaint your relationships after fire and smoke damage, you'd be wise to follow each step below.

The Next-Best Thing

We'd love to sit around your kitchen table, join you for coffee, and help you create a word picture. However, since the chances are slim we can do that, we'll do the next-best thing: We'll show you, step by step, how to tailor-make one to fit your needs. We'll do this by examining one of the most life-changing stories in history—the very one that generated the idea for this book!

Seven Steps to Creating Emotional Word Pictures

1. Establish a Clear Purpose.

To create effective word pictures, you must begin with an important preparatory step: deciding how you want to enrich your relationship. Do you want your words to:

A. Clarify thoughts and feelings?
B. Move you to a deeper level of intimacy?
C. Praise or encourage someone?
D. Lovingly correct someone?

Having a clear purpose in mind is like making a grocery list before you go shopping. The list helps guarantee you'll come home with what you need. In other words, shooting a gun without first aiming may work in Hollywood, but in real life you'll undoubtedly miss the target.

Why not take a moment right now and think about an important point you want to communicate with someone. Which of the four reasons will best help you deliver your message? To illustrate the need to have a clear purpose in mind, let's take a close look at a life-changing story.

Word pictures can help you clarify thoughts and feelings, move to a deeper level of intimacy, praise or encourage someone, or lovingly correct someone.

How would you like to be a royal adviser who was called upon to confront a warrior king—particularly one who had recently tried to cover up both an affair and first-degree murder? People who break "Watergates" of our day get rewarded with book and film contracts. However, in this adviser's day, exposing the truth was likely to get your neck broken. No word picture we know of better demonstrates the power to change a person's heart than the story of this ancient king.[1]

Solving a King-Sized Problem

There once was a young shepherd boy, named David, who was singled out to be a future king.[2] As a tender of flocks, he sometimes had to drive off wild animals and even lay his life on the line to save one of his sheep. But those years of leading a flock helped to develop many of the skills he later needed to lead a mighty nation.

When David finally ascended to the throne, he was known throughout the world as a fearless warrior who led his armies in countless victories.[3] He maintained the heart of a shepherd in the early years of his reign, but as his fame increased, he began walking on the dangerous edge of power. Anything he wanted was within his grasp.[4]

It was during this time, when his shepherd's heart had grown cold, that he walked onto the roof of his palace and gazed across the city at all he controlled, all he commanded. As the sun set and a refreshing breeze drifted down from the surrounding mountains, his eyes suddenly caught a reflection from a rooftop below. It was the last rays of sunlight, shimmering off a pool of water. Looking closer, he realized the reflection came as the water was stirred by a woman bathing.

Moving to a better vantage point, he scrutinized the beautiful woman. His pulse grew quicker; his breath, shorter. Then, his lust having devised a plan, he dispatched his guards to bring the woman to the palace. Soon enough, David learned that this striking woman, named Bathsheba, was the wife of one of his officers on the battle line.

However, that didn't deter David. His mind was not on a faraway battle but on a conquest near at hand. So he had her brought into his private chambers for a night of forbidden passion.

The next morning, the evening's entertainment was sent back home. There is every indication the king wanted their encounter to be a one-night stand—an act he could sweep under the carpet of his cold conscience. But several weeks later, the young woman sent a private message to the king. She was pregnant with his child.

In his early years, King David had been noted as an upright man. But by this time, his one error seemed to justify another. Perhaps he feared his grip on power would be loosened if people caught wind of the scandal. All we know is that instead of acknowledging what happened, his darkened heart devised another cunning plan.

He would send for the woman's husband, who was still away fighting, and bring him home on leave as a decorated hero. David was sure this soldier, like any average, red-blooded serviceman who'd been away from his beautiful wife for months, would fill his first night home with romance.

But Bathsheba's husband was several cuts above average. Since the men he commanded were still on the battle lines, far from their wives and families, he refused the privileges of marriage.

The king was stunned that the man's loyalty to his troops was more powerful than his passions. His mind quickly scrambled for a second plan, and a crude idea struck him. He invited him to the palace, got him drunk, and then sent him home. Yet once again, he refused to go inside. Knowing the wine would weaken his resolve, he slept on the steps of his house. Unbeknown to him, this put him in as much danger as being on the front lines. In fact, by spending another evening apart from his wife, he signed his own death certificate.

Several weeks had passed since Bathsheba first announced her pregnancy, and it took a few more to get her husband back from the battle. As a woman with a shapely figure, she couldn't keep the secret much longer. Increasingly desperate, David stooped the lowest when he grasped an evil plan that couldn't fail.

Through a top-secret dispatch, he sent her husband back to the front lines and into the thick of the battle. Then, following the king's specific instructions, the commanding general pulled back all his supporting troops to leave the soldier alone in the face of the enemy.

The plan worked flawlessly. With no protection on his flank and no one to stand with him, he battled bravely but futilely. Like a wounded stag encircled by starving wolves, he was slaughtered in the open, alone.

With Bathsheba's husband out of the way, the king brought his one-time lover into the palace as his new wife. Overnight, a thin veneer of legitimacy covered the dark secret. In time, David's fears of being found out relaxed. He slept much easier, knowing there had been additional casualties on the front and that many of the widows had also remarried. He desperately hoped the general who executed his evil sentence would guard the secret with his life. However, the truth somehow leaked out.

Powerful Words That Pierce the Heart

While King David's conscience had been in hiding, a court adviser named Nathan was given a divine charge. He was to confront David with an emotional word picture that would change the course of a kingdom and echo throughout the ages.

"Your Majesty," his adviser began, bowing low, "a serious problem in the kingdom has just come to my attention."

After listening to dozens of everyday reports from other advisers, David suddenly snapped awake. Like most kings, he didn't appreciate surprises—particularly serious ones affecting *his* kingdom.

"Sir, in your kingdom is a very poor family, who with all their resources could purchase only one suckling lamb," he began, weighing each word for its emotional impact. "And as this animal grew, the children took over the chores of feeding and brushing it.

"The lamb became a special pet and an important part of the household," he continued. "In fact, they were so attached to it that they gave it the run of the house. At night, when the winds blew, it even jumped onto the children's beds and helped keep them warm.

"In this poor family, the father farms land owned by a wealthy rancher," he said. "Recently, late in the afternoon, unexpected guests arrived at the rich man's house. A customary feast was in order. Yet the herdsmen were away with the flocks, and the only fresh meat at hand was one of the aging goats kept for their milk—far too tough a meal for the important guests.

"That's when the landowner looked down the hill and saw two children playing with a beautiful, plump lamb," the adviser said, pausing momentarily to clear his throat.

"Well, go on," the king replied impatiently. "Finish your story."

"Yes, Your Majesty," he said, maintaining his voice at its deliberate pace. "As I was saying, the rich man saw the animal, and an idea came to him. He could butcher the lamb and not have to send a servant all the way to his own flocks. And that's exactly what he did. The lamb was slaughtered and prepared for his guests, without any thought given to the children or their parents."

Color rushed to the king's face, and his eyes flashed with rage. His feelings brought back memories, which in turn sparked deeper feelings. He, too, had raised lambs from birth, sheltered them from harm, loved them as pets, and felt heartbroken if anything happened to them.

"As you know, Your Majesty, children may have the heart for battle, but they are no match for grown men. With their father away tending his fields, their cries for help went unheard. And the little boy, clinging desperately to the lamb, was slapped away like a fly.

"That night, the little children huddled in their beds, weeping to hear the music and laughter from the rancher's house above. Their hearts broke to think of other people's appetites being satisfied by the pet which—"

"That's enough!" the king shouted. "Say no more!" He jumped to his feet, livid with anger. "That man deserves death! I tell you, today he is to make restitution to that family. He is to pay them back fourfold what they lost. I want four of his best lambs to be chosen from his flocks, and I want them taken to that family—immediately," he commanded, hammering out the words. "And then," he said, with a glint in his eyes that reflected the warrior's heart within, "I want that man brought before me this very afternoon!"

The large throne room had the acoustics of a Gothic church. When the king's angry words ceased reverberating from the walls, a heavy silence fell upon the room. Ears were poised with anticipation. Though the adviser never spoke above a whisper, the impact of his words crashed through the room like peals of thunder.

"Your Majesty," he began, *"you* are that man! The little lamb you took was another man's wife!"

The story hit the king so forcefully and unexpectedly that he was driven to his knees. His heart, encased by adultery and murder in steel-like silence, now lay shattered by the blow of one emotional word picture. For the first time, he was forced to face the evil he had done, forced to *feel* some of the emotional trauma he had caused others.[5]

You may not have to face an angry king anytime soon, but you probably are aware of someone with whom you need to talk. Like Nathan, you may need to confront a problem in a relationship. Correction may not be the easiest of the four primary uses of word pictures, and it often takes the most courage. But when done in love to change a destructive practice or situation, it is frequently the most important. On the other hand, perhaps you're looking for more clarity in your communication or greater intimacy in your marriage. Maybe you're searching for just the right words of love and encouragement for your children.

Whether your relationships need a major overhaul or you simply want to add a turbocharger to your communication, the solution is near at hand. As we've seen, the first step in creating a word picture is to consider its purpose. As we highlight the six remaining steps, you'll see how quickly and easily you can develop word pictures that can make history in your home.

CHAPTER SIX

Creating an Effective Emotional Word Picture

PART TWO

If you're like most people, you're probably postponing a conversation or two because you're not quite sure how best to express your feelings. Perhaps you're headed into your boss's office to fight once more for a raise, or you need to talk to your teenager about her dress code (or lack of one). Maybe you've got to explain to your wife, for the third time, that you need to switch vacation dates, or to discuss with your husband, for the third time, the family chaos that comes with making that switch.

If you have a needed conversation in mind, first isolate your communication goal. Then you're ready to take the second crucial step.

2. Carefully Study the Other Person's Interests.

The word picture used with King David showed an intimate understanding of his background and interests. That is, Nathan chose a story that tapped into David's experience as a shepherd and a defender of his people. By doing so, Nathan took a shortcut to the king's heart.

The same is true of Kimberly's word picture that helped bring her father back home. All her life, she'd watched him take immaculate care of his company car to impress new clients. By tapping into his lifelong love affair with automobiles, she effectively parked her story of a wrecked car right on the doorstep of his heart.

It may take some detective work to discover your listener's interests, but even the most hard-core television addicts, "couch potatoes," or "lounge lizards" give you clues about their lives. Your listener may be a person whose problem behavior can be short-circuited by linking your word picture with his or her favorite television program!

Research another person's past, and don't neglect the present. Discover what he enjoyed as a child; what he hates as an adult; the sports, hobbies, food, or music he prefers; the car he drives and how he keeps it; what he does for recreation; and what motivates him to work overtime.

The same thing is true if you're researching a word picture for a woman. Learn enough about her world to understand what makes her good days good and bad days terrible. If she works at home, what are her needs and frustrations? If she works outside, what does she do during lunch breaks?

Again, your search for clues—for men or women— may take minor investigative work and draw you into areas you know nothing about. But don't quit until you've uncovered an interest that can support a word picture.

For me (Gary), the search for the key to my youngest son's heart took me to a swinging place.

Breaking Old Habits

When Michael was thirteen, I felt I needed to talk with him about his eating habits. Frankly, he was eating so much junk food that I thought he'd be targeted as a cleanup site by the Environmental Protection Agency. With the goal of communicating that concern to him, I began hunting for one of his current interests. Since we'd just bought him a new set of golf clubs, I had a major clue to what that might be.

We live in Phoenix, and the *Arizona Golf Course Directory* lists 108 courses in the metropolitan area. The weather permits you to play at least 360 days a year, and it's close to being golf heaven. Yet like the person who lives next to the ocean but never goes in the water, I rarely get my golf balls wet in the lakes of the local courses. But that all changed when I saw Michael's new clubs and realized what a major inroad they were into his heart.

When I suggested that we go golfing, Mike jumped at the idea. He was more than thrilled to thrash me on the links, and he even tried to convince me to double his allowance if he beat me by ten strokes.

Once on the course, I noticed that Mike was continually slicing the ball. While he worked to improve his handicap, I was replacing the huge divots I plowed with each swing. We'd each played better, but we still had a great father-son time and finished the front nine holes in a tie.

As we waited on the back nine for round two, I again rehearsed the word picture that I felt sure would capture my son's attention. As we sat watching a foursome ahead of us tee off, I turned to Michael.

"Hey, big guy," I said, "have you ever heard of Jack Nicklaus?"

"Of course, Dad. Everyone who's picked up a club knows about the 'Golden Bear.'"

"Well, if he were playing with us today," I said, "would you listen if he explained how you could get rid of your slice?"

"You bet I would!"

"Well, Michael, I'm not Jack Nicklaus, but you know I love you and want the best for you, don't you?"

"Sure, Dad. But what does that have to do with my golf swing?"

As I looked at him, I could see his mind racing back and forth, trying to guess what I was getting at. "Did you know that in one area of your life I see you doing something that's like slicing every shot into the woods? It's such a problem, it could actually slow you down in life, cause you to have an earlier death, and even keep you off the golf course for good."

"What do you mean?" he asked, a puzzled look clouding his face. "What am I doing that's so bad?"

"Michael, every day I watch you ignoring the advice of experts in the field of medicine. These men and women are as good at what they do as Jack Nicklaus is at golfing. Yet every time I talk to you about your eating habits, I feel resistance, not a receptive attitude."

I picked up his driver and held it in my hand. "Eating so much junk food is like gripping your club the wrong way and refusing to change your swing. It's like having Jack Nicklaus standing next to you, showing you how to change your swing, but still refusing to take his advice.

"Mike, if Jack Nicklaus were here today, he'd point out things that would help you be the best. I mention this because I want you to enjoy the healthiest life you possibly can."

I could see in his face that my word picture hit home—all because I'd tapped into one of his major interests. Plus our conversation provided a springboard for further discussion about how his junk-food diet was slicing away his shot at a healthy life.

My purpose in taking Michael golfing was not to manipulate him. Rather, I became a student of his interests out of love. I wanted the best for Michael—not me. Before, my words of warning had been received, at best, as a lecture. But as we sat on the golf course that Saturday, Michael clearly saw and *felt* the concern behind my words. While I can't say he instantly corrected his eating habits, his attitude about discussing them did change immediately. And in the months ahead, I found fewer and fewer hamburger cartons and Snickers wrappers littering his room.

We know there are limits on how much you can research another person's interests. It may be quite impractical for you to take up needlepoint or professional wrestling, and you may have no inclination to study nuclear physics. But if you look long and hard enough, you'll discover the interests that enable you to enter the world of the person you're trying to reach . . . and move on to the next step.

3. Draw from Four Inexhaustible Wells.

Many people experience a common initial reaction when considering the use of word pictures: "Wait a minute, I'm not creative! It would take a miracle for me to come up with a story that works." Actually, you don't have to worry about how creative you are. Believe it or not, you've been hearing and *using* word pictures for years.

Every time you sing the national anthem, you're singing a word picture. Before every ball game and school function, Francis Scott Key paints vivid patriotic pictures with lyrics, such as "the rockets' red glare, the bombs bursting in air. . . ." And if you've ever listened to a country music station—accidentally or on purpose—you've heard nonstop word pictures, including "I don't mind the thorns, if you're the rose," "She done stomped on my heart, and mashed that sucker flat," and "Don't it make your brown eyes blue?"

Interestingly, the root meanings of many everyday words can be traced to word pictures. For example, the Hebrew word for anger originally meant "red nostrils."[1] That's because when someone gets mad, blood rushes to the face and their nostrils flare. Likewise, the original Hebrew meaning of our word *fear* is derived from the word for "kidneys."[2] If someone has ever jumped out at you in the dark, you *know* why this part of our anatomy was used as a word picture!

In addition to the above, you've probably been using dozens of "mini word pictures" for years without realizing it. For example, have you ever heard or said: "Be careful—he's a wolf in sheep's clothing," "She's just pulling your leg," "He's a sight for sore eyes," "I lead a dog's life," "We're stuck in a rut," "He proved it beyond a shadow of a doubt," "They're just keeping up with the Joneses," "He's always selling people short," "It looks like a long shot," "They're like peas from the same pod," "It's just not going to pan out," "She'd stand up to him if she had any backbone," "He was as red as a beet," "She was as white as a sheet," or "That was a close shave"?

Or have you ever said: "Their baby is cute as a button," "He doesn't seem to have both oars in the water," "She's as skinny as a beanpole," "He's a chip off the old block," "They're taking us on a wild-goose chase," "Her lights are on, but no one's home," "She's got a chip on her shoulder," "My supervisor has a yellow streak a mile wide," "It was mashed flatter than a pancake," "He's nice, but the elevator doesn't reach the top floor," or "It's time to quit with all these examples and get the ball rolling"?

Do you *get the picture*—that creating word pictures

might not be as difficult as you think? It's not hard to find a meaningful one to use—if you know where to look. As you read through the next four chapters, you'll discover four bottomless wells that are full of emotional word pictures. One well is filled with nature and its wonders. Another is packed with everyday objects. A third contains imaginary stories, while the fourth plunges deeply into past experiences and re-membrances.

Kimberly chose her word picture from the Well of Everyday Objects. In her case, her father's interest in automobiles led her right to this well. The royal adviser, Nathan, drew from the Well of Imaginary Stories, sparking David's memories of his life as a shepherd boy.

Chapters 7 through 10 will thoroughly explain each of these wells. But with the introduction we've had to them, we're now ready for the fourth step—an impor-tant stage that, if ignored, can prevent your communi-cation efforts from reaching their full height of effectiveness.

4. Rehearse Your Story.

Over the years, we've learned that practice *does* make perfect. Rehearsing your story pays big divi-dends. Failing to do so robs it of its potential power.

We didn't know until long after Kimberly sent her letter, but she rewrote her father's word picture more than a dozen times. With each revision, she picked out some new aspect of a car wreck that illustrated the hurt and pain her family felt.

We're not suggesting you must write down all your word pictures in advance. We seldom do. In many situations, it's not practical or even possible. But time and again, we've seen tremendous benefits to thor-oughly researching and carefully thinking through a story.

As former athletes, we also recommend that you work with a coach. If word pictures are as new to your friend as they are to you, at least get someone to be your cheering section! Practicing with another person boosts your confidence and provides additional insights that you'll find tremendously helpful when the big moment arrives. So if you're serious about having your words achieve your desired purpose, call for a backup. Doing so will help maximize the impact of your word picture and build a stronger bond between you and your friend.

As we trace back over the path to creating a word picture, we've taken four important steps. We've chosen a clear purpose for communicating, focused on an area of the other person's interest, drawn an object or story from one of four overflowing wells, and carefully practiced what we want to say. Now it's time to consider the fifth step: the issue of timing.

5. Pick a Convenient Time Without Distractions.

We recently spoke at a two-day, marriage-enrichment conference. The first night, we briefly discussed emotional word pictures. The next morning, just before the opening session when we were to talk in detail about the concept, a woman stormed up to tell us our "wild idea" didn't work.

"I went home and tried your dumb word-picture method with my husband last night, and I can tell you for a fact it doesn't work," she charged, beginning to pick up steam. "You ought to make a public statement this morning, telling everybody to forget about using it. In fact, *give me that microphone.* I'll make the announcement myself!"

Luckily, the microphone wasn't on yet, and we were able to calm her down enough to discover what went wrong. As we listened to her story, we realized she didn't understand any of the steps to creating word pictures—particularly step five, choosing the right time and setting. She had merely gotten excited about the concept, loaded both barrels of her verbal gun, and blasted away at her husband the second she walked in the door.

This woman certainly had legitimate concerns about her marriage. She was distraught that her husband had decided, at the last moment, to stay home and watch a football game instead of attending the marriage seminar. When push came to shove, he cared more about who won the game than the respect he'd lose in her eyes. So when she caught the scent of how word pictures could improve a marriage, she took off like a hungry park bear and smashed down every door in trying them on her husband.

"Why don't you tell us exactly what happened," we said.

"Well, my husband was watching another of his dumb football games when I got home last night," she began. "It was even a game he'd taped from the week before! I was so mad I thought up a word picture on the spot.

"'Edward,' I said, turning off the television and standing in front of it, 'do you know what you make me feel like when you're watching your dumb games? Do you?'

"I told him, 'I feel like a crumb on the kitchen table that is lying there from dinner. As if that's not bad enough, you come by on your way to watch TV and brush me off onto the floor. And if that's still not bad enough, the dog comes along and licks me right up! Now, what do you think of *that?*'"

"What happened next?" we asked.

"He just looked at me as if I were drunk. Finally, he shook his head and said, 'What do *I* think of that? I think that's a *dumb* way to feel, that's what I think! Now, turn that television set back on, and get out of my way!' And with that, he went right back to watching his game!"

The woman had created a word picture with great expectations. We suspect that at the very least, she thought her husband would instantly fall to his knees and beg her forgiveness for ignoring her in the past, and then smash his television set into a thousand pieces with the remote control unit.

Yet that didn't happen. They moved even further apart. Why? She had nailed down the first step in creating a word picture: clarifying her purpose. That is, she wanted to hammer her husband with words and nail him right where he sat! She was in such a hurry that she couldn't even wait until halftime. In effect, she'd tossed the turkey into the oven without reading the instructions. Consequently, her results went up in smoke.

She erred because her timing was wrong. She conveyed her message at the worst possible moment, and she hadn't taken the time to tap into his interests or draw from the well that best pictured them. After all, his primary interest was obvious. It was twenty-one inches diagonally, and his face was glued to it. This man was a TVaholic and a football fanatic. A world of sports word pictures could have tackled him and thrown his insensitive actions for a loss. It's no wonder her words never reached his heart. He couldn't relate to a crumb falling off the table.

Another mistake was that she took absolutely no time to practice her word picture. Granted, it can sometimes be as hard to hold back our words as it is to stop an onrushing lineman. Nevertheless, she needed practice to get her words in shape and a friend to encourage or coach her. That would have involved more effort, of course, but it would have been better than having her words slammed back in her face. By neglecting to practice and plan an effective game strategy, she lost her offensive weapon and was knocked from contention before she was able to score.

Picking the right time and place to convey a word picture is a key to its effective use.

With all the athletic imagery we've used, it's obvious the woman could have chosen a sports-related word picture. Though she may have known nothing about football, she could have sought out a coach and learned enough about the game to meet her husband on familiar turf. But there's more to effective communication than selecting the right field of interest and then practicing. Picking the right time and place to convey a word picture is also a key to its effective use.

Again, take Kimberly as an example. There was never a good time for her to talk with her father. He slammed the door to serious conversation on his few visits and took his phone off the hook every night. So she delivered her message in the mail. Kimberly knew he reserved an unhurried time to go through his letters. And by choosing the right moment and setting to present her word picture, her planning paid off—as it did for Nathan, who waited until the opportune moment to confront King David.[3]

If your story is to be most effective, it must be given at a well-thought-out time and place. The rewards of a highly crafted word picture don't come by blurting out our thoughts of the moment. They come from engaging our minds before we engage our mouths.

6. Try and Try Again.

In the case of both Kimberly and Nathan, the very first word picture they used won the desired result. However, in some cases it may take more than one before the other person genuinely hears our thoughts and feelings. The better we become at steps two and three (becoming a student of someone's interests and choosing from one of the four wells), the more our first word pictures will hit their marks. But if they don't, don't panic. Reload and try again!

In another of our books, *The Blessing,* we relayed the story of a woman who couldn't stand the house she lived in.[4] Even though she and her husband easily could have afforded a nicer home, she couldn't convince her husband to move, despite years of trying.

Whenever the discussion came up, he'd explain away her feelings and make his own case for staying put. Even a word picture she devised fell on deaf ears. But instead of quitting, she went back to the drawing board, picked out another of his interests, and tried a second one. And then a third.

What we didn't mention in our previous book was that it took four attempts before she finally caught his attention. The earlier tries may have failed because he didn't understand them, or perhaps the timing wasn't right. Maybe his wife simply didn't capture an interest that lay close enough to his heart. Whatever the reason, her fourth story about a fish in a rusty barrel hooked him.

He was so moved by what she said that he promptly got up from his chair, called a Realtor-friend, and put the house on the market. Then he pulled out his checkbook. "Is this enough to start construction of the home you want?" he asked, handing her a check— that would clear the bank with room to spare—for $150,000.

The woman's persistence with word pictures got her a new house. Naturally, we won't claim that similar perseverance will enable you to move into a nicer home. But we can assure you that you'll get results if you don't quit. We've seen persistence pay off in other ways: for a woman who landed a job with a company that had turned her down twice before; for another woman who gained an extra five days of vacation time after repeated requests; for the parents who finally convinced a teenager to spend more time with his younger brother; and for a teacher who eventually helped a shy grade-schooler begin reaching out to her classmates.

We live in an instant society, where we expect all food to be microwaveable and all prime-time shows to conclude with a happy ending in twenty-five minutes and ten commercials. But real life doesn't always work that way. There are times when you can't get another person to understand what you're saying on the first try, or when you're still at loggerheads despite your initial hard work to craft the right picture. But don't give up! In the real world, a key to communication is being lovingly persistent.

Granted, it's frustrating not to get instantaneous results when we use a word picture. But some people could be pummeled by a hundred of the most powerful word pictures and not feel a single blow. In fact, we've devoted a later chapter to that small group of people who seem totally unaffected by them.[5] But please don't race ahead and label your "resistant" person as being in this camp without giving persistence every chance to pay off.

We must stress that over the years we've seen very few people who are so emotionally, mentally, and spiritually callous that they cannot be reached by word pictures. We've even seen "impossible cases" — where a husband or wife has insisted his or her spouse was beyond hope—be changed dramatically through the language of love.

So don't be discouraged if you run into an occasional "What a dumb way to feel!" In almost every case, your loving patience will enable you to reach new heights of communication with your friend, associate, or relative. While up there, put the seventh and final step into practice.

7. Milk Your Word Picture for All It's Worth!

What in the world do we mean by "milking" a word picture? Try thinking of it in these terms: Once you've gotten one light turned on with your word picture, flip on every switch in the house! For example, we once worked with a woman who was extremely frustrated about her personal life. After working for years in a career she loved, she married and had children relatively late in life. She had a strong marriage and deeply loved her twin baby daughters. But sometimes she battled with her emotions over her decision to resign her job to be home with her girls.

"I know I shouldn't feel this way," she said. "Still, I sometimes feel like a bird in a cage. I really love it inside, and I know how important it is for my baby birds to have a secure place in which to grow. But at times I feel like breaking open the cage and flying out!"

Her word picture conveyed a great deal of insight about her frustrations, and we could have let it stand on its own. But suspecting there was more to the story, we asked a series of follow-up questions that "milked" her word picture for additional meaning: "If you flew out of the cage, where would you go?" we asked. "How long would you be gone? Is your husband in the cage with you, or do you see him flying free somewhere else?"

When we asked this last question about her husband, it was as if we had opened the floodgate to some emotional dam she had been building inside. Suddenly, months of frustration spilled out.

In a rush of words, she explained that her husband was an only child whose sole premarriage experience with youngsters was watching other people's children from a distance. Though he had been eager to start a family, deep down he felt insecure as a parent. As a result, he unconsciously avoided being at home. The more time he spent at work, the less he was able to provide physical and emotional support for his wife and twins. And within only a few months, his lack of care had begun taking its toll on their relationship.

Had we not taken the time to milk her word picture, we might have let her go with a few encouraging words, such as "Thanks for being so honest with your feelings. Probably every young mother occasionally feels as if she's in a cage, particularly when her twin daughters have just had their shots and are teething as well!"

But milking her story helped us (and her) clarify her concerns, better understand her husband's fears, and catch a problem that could have led to a major breakdown. She later told us that one of the first things her husband did after hearing her expanded word picture was to ask, "Honey, what could I do to open the cage and help you get out and exercise your wings?"

By bringing more issues and feelings to the surface, you, too, will discover new depth in your relationships and additional benefits in your conversations. It's possible if you milk your word pictures for all they're worth.

At this point, we have examined all seven steps to creating and using word pictures:

1. Establish a clear purpose.
2. Carefully study the other person's interests.
3. Draw from four inexhaustible wells.
4. Rehearse your story.
5. Pick a convenient time without distractions.

6. Try and try again.
7. Milk your word picture for all it's worth.

You should now have a good grasp of how to use this dynamic communication tool in your most meaningful relationships. But knowing how to create effective word pictures isn't enough. You must also know where to find them. An inexhaustible source is near at hand in the four bottomless wells mentioned earlier. They provide an unending supply of word power, as one husband found when he drew from the Well of Nature to stop his wife's steady stream of nagging and critical words.

FOUR
INEXHAUSTIBLE
WELLS
FILLED WITH
WORD
PICTURES

CHAPTER SEVEN

The Well of Nature

Jim knew he needed help with a problem that was crippling his marriage and causing problems with his children. Yet who would have thought that an object from the Well of Nature could have brought such dramatic changes?

This husband crafted one story that halted his wife's criticism. In fact, his word picture was so powerful that we have used it in counseling many other couples and have seen it deeply affect their lives.

By drawing from the inexhaustible Well of Nature, you, too, can utilize all the created world around you to increase your word power. Animals, weather, mountains, water, and hundreds of other natural elements can provide the entrance ticket to another person's heart, just as Jim discovered.

Turning the Tide of Criticism

As a high-school teacher and football coach, Jim rarely saw his house in broad daylight. That had its advantages. By going to work before dawn and coming home after dark, the peeling paint and overgrown weeds conveniently disappeared.

Though Jim's annual sacrifice for gridiron glory caused the house to suffer somewhat, he tried to make sure his family didn't. Each night possible, he carved out time for horsey rides and snatches of conversation with the kids. However, there seldom was enough time left over for his wife, Susan.

By drawing from the inexhaustible Well of Nature, you can utilize the world around you to increase your word power.

After the kids were in bed, he would hole up alone in the den to spend long hours studying films of the next week's opponent. And morning always came too soon. In fact, the interval between setting the alarm clock and being jolted awake seemed to be measured in nanoseconds.

Before long, the lack of time spent with her husband began grating on Susan. By nature she never strayed more than three steps from her daily planner. (One look at it and any "Big 8" accounting firm would have hired her on the spot.) Her every move was charted by the hour, and she couldn't understand why Jim couldn't do the same thing. Indeed, the fluctuations of his schedule rocked her carefully structured life—especially each fall when the football season showed up on the calendar.

Every year that he coached, her frustration level soared higher than the football field bleachers. The more his schedule varied, the more critical she became. Like an uninvited guest who doesn't know when to go home, her disapproval wouldn't budge.

Jim tried everything to dislodge her bitter attitude

toward the demands of his job: lectures, logic, even a few screaming threats. After all, he was a football coach and had played ball himself at a major university. He knew how to be loud. But he also recognized that his lectures and tough-as-nails approach failed miserably to change her behavior. In desperation, he finally resorted to the word picture technique he'd heard us discuss at a conference for educators.

The following night, Jim returned home from practice. The moment he entered the house, he spotted their four-month-old golden retriever. Cracker was a beautiful puppy that his wife loved dearly. As the dog scampered up to him wagging its tail, he realized he'd found a key to his wife's emotions.

For the first time, he felt he had something *new* to say instead of expressing the same stale thoughts again and again at different volume settings.

So far, he had followed the playbook step by step for creating an effective word picture.[1] He'd carefully chosen a clear communication purpose and had picked something close to her heart. What's more, he waited to practice his word picture—drawn from the Well of Nature—the next day after school with a close friend. Then, armed with his new communication tool, he prepared to share the story with Susan.

The children were in bed, and Jim had just turned off the late-night news. He knew that an important part of getting his word picture across was picking an unhurried time to express the message. And with three sons, the house would never be quieter. Predictably, Cracker was stationed at her favorite place in life, curled beside Susan's feet.

"Honey," he said, "let's have a talk."

"It's late," came her cool reply. "I don't know if I'm up to talking about anything right now."

"It won't take long. I just want to tell you a story about how I've been feeling lately."

Rarely did Jim offer to express anything even remotely resembling a feeling, so Susan nodded and sat back in her chair.

"Honey, I guess I've been feeling . . . well, sort of like Cracker probably felt when she was living with your grandfather over on the farm before we got her.

"I've got hunting blood in my veins, and I want to run, explore, and roam so badly!" he continued. "But I've been left in the fenced backyard, and spend most of my time walking in circles while chained to a tree.

"Well, one day I'm left unleashed and curiosity gets the best of me. So I dig a hole under the fence and sneak out. Like a shot out of a gun, I dash far into the woods. The problem is, I'm so excited about getting to run free that I don't realize I'm getting farther and farther from the house.

"All of a sudden, I look around and my heart sinks. Without realizing it, I've gone so deep into the woods that I'm lost—really lost. I search like mad to find a path back home. But every trail leads to a dead end or takes me farther from where I want to be. I spend the entire day trying to find my way back to Grandpa's, but instead I run into nothing but trouble.

"In the morning, I get chased by a pack of coyotes; in the afternoon, I'm nearly run over by a logging truck; about dusk, I fall into a dirty stream—the only water I can find to drink. By the end of the day, my paws are cut and bleeding, and I'm wet, exhausted, and scared."

With a quick glance at Susan, he could see that her attention was riveted to the story.

"Late that night, I finally stumble onto another trail. After having walked through the darkest woods I've seen, I suddenly spot some familiar landmarks.

Sure enough, I recognize a trail I know will take me right back to Grandpa's house. Despite how tired and sore I am, I start running down the path. My legs carry me faster and faster. My heart pounds when I finally see the driveway, and I struggle the last few yards to the fence.

"I want to see Grandpa so much and to feel safe and warm again. I look around for the hole I had dug that morning and squeeze under it. Then, with my last ounce of strength, I crawl over to the back door and scratch on the screen. As tired as I am, I yelp and bark for the door to be opened. I can hardly wait for somebody to hold me, dry me off, and feed me.

"Just then, the back porch light goes on. I'm so excited, thinking, *At last, I'm with my family. Somebody's finally going to comfort me instead of chasing me. There's going to be fresh water to drink, food to eat, and . . .*

"Instead of any of that happening," Jim said, pausing a moment to let his words sink in, "the screen door is thrown open, and I'm knocked back down the stairs. Before I can get up, a stick about three feet long whacks me on the side. I'm already hurt and tired from being lost all day, but now I feel even more pain and confusion as I'm chased around the yard, being hit again and again. All the while, I hear an angry voice yelling, 'If you *ever* run away again, this is nothing compared to what's going to happen to you!' But all I can do is think, *I've worked so hard to get home, and now I'm being whipped!*

"He finally catches me, puts me on a long chain that's fastened to an iron post, and leaves me until morning in the cold and dew without anything to eat or drink. It's supposed to be a lesson, I'm sure. But it rips my heart out and makes me think running away wasn't so bad after all."

Jim paused again, and the room was as quiet as an empty church. "Susan, you probably don't realize it, but that's how I feel most evenings when I come home. You see, I really enjoy coaching and teaching, but by the end of the day I'm worn out. If it isn't something one of my students has done or another teacher has said, it's having a bad practice or losing a game.

"It's rough working all those hours with so little in return. During the day, I'm always thinking that I can hardly wait to return to my own backyard—back to the kids, back to you, back to those I want so much to hug me, tell me they love me, and assure me everything is all right. I need you to tell me that you love me and that you're proud of me—even if I'm not a perfect husband and father.

"But Susan, most evenings when I walk up to the door, instead of getting hugged, I get hit with sarcasm or critical words, such as 'You have time to do everything *you* want, why don't you have time to fix the one thing *I* want fixed?' or 'I asked you to bring home *wheat* bread, not *white*. Why can't you ever remember what I tell you?' or 'If you've got time to coach *everybody else's* kids, why aren't you spending more time with *your own?*' and on and on and on.

"Your words are like whips that sting me over and over. When I try to respond or get things on a better footing, you hit me with your critical words in the bedroom, chase me into the kitchen, and follow me outside. And if I raise my arm to ward off a blow, you strike my hand or elbow.

"Susan, I'm so covered with welts from what you've said to me that I just want to spend more time in the woods at school. It's lonely there, and I have to dodge a few coyotes and logging trucks. But at least I'm not hit by your critical words.

"Honey, I know you've got legitimate reasons to be upset about my schedule during the season. I don't like having to work so much, either. But this problem is really beginning to affect our relationship. I can see it having a negative impact every day, and the kids notice, too.

"I don't know how else to tell you, but when it comes to our marriage, I feel like little Cracker returning to something other than 'home, sweet home' after being lost all day in the woods."

Jim surprised himself at the amount of emotion that came out in telling the story, but he was even more shocked by his wife's reaction. Susan was so moved by the story that she wept uncontrollably for almost half an hour.

Later, Susan told us, "For years, I'd known I was overly critical of Jim and said a lot of hurtful things. But until he told me the story, I had no idea how my words affected him. He even felt bad for telling it to me, and afterward he hugged me and told me he was sorry for bringing it up. But I was so touched by his word picture that all I could do was cry.

"I'm not exactly sure why I *felt* his story so intensely, but it changed me," she continued. "That night I decided my attitude toward Jim was wrong. Even though I had previously rationalized it in my mind, I knew I was hitting him too often and much too hard with my words. I was angry because I couldn't see him more. But all my complaining was pushing him farther away from me, not drawing him closer.

"It's still a struggle for me to flex so much during the football season, and each fall we still have to talk through those frustrations," she said. "But I made an important decision that night. Whenever Jim comes home, no matter how late he is or how frustrated I am, he'll never again be met with a stick."

Cracker never realized she was serving as "man's best friend" simply by lying at Susan's feet, but Jim did. And in using the puppy as the basis of his word picture, he selected just one of thousands of illustrations from the Well of Nature.

Like Jim, you can draw from this well when it best suits another person's interests. Let's look at three other people who dipped into the Well of Nature to make a positive difference in their relationships. These examples will give you a quick, snapshot glimpse of how they used the language of love to confront an insensitive guest, rekindle lost love, and honor a special friend.

Confronting an Insensitive Guest

"Jayne, we're both from Minnesota, right? Remember what it's like to wait and wait for spring?" Beth said to her houseguest, who was staying with her temporarily until the movers could get her settled into her new condo. "Remember how tired you got shoveling snow from your driveway, knowing that people in Florida were basking in the sun? Can you remember how excited you were to see the barren trees budding after a long winter's sleep?

"Jayne, you probably don't realize it, but shortly after you arrived to stay in our home, I heard you say something that really hurt me. It made me feel as if I was living back in Minnesota and heard that spring would be postponed six months—that I'd have to endure another half-year of ice, snow, and freezing wind.

"Let me tell you what you said that affected me that way . . ."

Longing for Lost Intimacy

"Brian, can we talk a few minutes before we head out on our jog?" Claudia said, sitting on the edge of the bed as her husband tied his shoes. "You need to know that I've been feeling as if we've been running along side by side on our favorite jogging course— you know, the cedar-chip path that winds through all those beautiful homes and down through the park.

"Running that course is fun for both of us. We're able to talk while we jog, there aren't any big dogs roaming around, and the exercise is doing us a lot of good.

"But lately, I feel as if every time we start to jog, we run into a big detour sign that forces us to take a path other than our favorite. Instead of running past the pretty houses, we're dodging traffic on busy streets. And instead of jogging down to the park and back, we're struggling up gravel hills.

"Brian, I used to really enjoy running with you. But now I feel as if the path we're running on is covered with rocks. It's just a matter of time before one of us stumbles or falls or worse.

"I need to tell you why I think that detour sign went up and why we're headed down such a rocky road . . ."

Honoring a Special Friend

"Hey, Don. Have a minute?" Bob said, taking a few quick steps to catch up with his coworker. "I just want to thank you for last week. I know you think it was no big deal, but let me illustrate how much I appreciated your help by telling you a story.

"We're both golfers, right? At least we call ourselves golfers! Anyway, about three months ago when the boss gave me that new assignment, I felt as if I was put in charge of the course that would be used for the Masters' Golf Tournament. It was a tremendous opportunity, and I was thrilled at the honor. But you know as well as I that I'd never taken care of a golf course in my life.

"Well, Don, I feel you took time you didn't really have to teach me how to care for that course. You showed me how high to mow the grass in the fairways and the best way to cut the greens. You taught me when to water, where to place the sprinklers, and how much water to use.

"I put in the hours all right, but you helped me know where those hours needed to go. And when the tournament was over and all the pros were walking around raving about the course, you were the one I wanted to call and thank."

These are but a fraction of the ways you can use a word picture from the Well of Nature to go straight to a person's heart. Like those we've written about, we've seen many people draw from this well to make an important difference in another person's life.

We've known a single parent who turned her teenage son's attitude around by talking to him about a backyard tree; a father who brought everyone to tears at his daughter's wedding rehearsal with his story of a beautiful butterfly; and a son who explained to his parents how he felt about leaving for college, using the image of a small creek that had grown over the years into a strong river.

While the Well of Nature is a tremendous source for life-changing word pictures, there are three other wells from which to draw. In fact, we think one of the most exciting parts of this book is the overwhelming potential for meaningful communication found in these four wells.

In the next chapter, we'll watch Susan draw from the Well of Everyday Objects to gain the deepest desire of her heart: more time with her husband. And though it was never her intention, her word picture splashed over and changed our lives also.

CHAPTER EIGHT

The Well of
Everyday Objects

In the previous chapter, we saw how Jim's word picture from the Well of Nature brought a dramatic halt to his wife's critical words. It's now time to read about . . . the *rest* of the story.

The day after Jim spoke with Susan, he couldn't wait to call our office and to boast about the changes in their marriage. For weeks afterward, we heard his glowing reports about how Susan was making an all-out effort to take the sharp edge off her words and tone of voice.

Just as we were preparing to recommend them for a congressional marriage citation for "Most Dramatic Turnaround," Jim showed up unexpectedly at our office when John was at a conference. Jim's eyes and nonverbal actions screamed that something was bothering him. I offered him a cup of coffee, which he politely but firmly refused.

"Gary, I'd like to talk with you a few minutes if I can," he said.

No sooner had I ushered him into my office and shut the door than he verbally pounced on me.

"Thanks a lot," he said. "You know your word picture method has really helped us. For the first time in years, I feel Susan understands me. She's made some dramatic improvements this past month. She's even telling me things she appreciates about me instead of criticizing me."

Jim paused, as if waiting for me to say something.

"Well, that doesn't sound too bad!" I replied, hoping this was all that was coming but knowing it wasn't.

"Yeah, well that's only part of the story," he said. "A week ago, Susan asked if she could share a word picture with me. What she said stunned me so badly it brought tears to my eyes, and I still haven't gotten over it.

"I don't know how I've missed the problem for so many years. But now I understand what's been at the heart of her frustration with me. It makes perfect sense! Now I can see why she's been on my case so much.

"Let me tell you," Jim said, shaking his head. "I've had some kind of a week mulling things over. That word picture stays with me night and day, and it beats me up emotionally whenever I think about it."

Straightening up in his chair and looking at me with a twinkle in his eye, he said, "I thought you were my friend, Smalley. Thanks a lot!"

By focusing on an area of Jim's interest and choosing the best time to talk, Susan turned the tables on Jim. The hunted became the hunter, and she had lined up in her sights a blind spot in Jim's life.

Jim went on to recount the word picture his wife had given him, drawn from the Well of Everyday Objects.

As I listened to the story, my eyes were opened to an

overlooked issue in my own marriage. Like Jim, I wasn't consciously trying to cause any problems at home. However, I was consistently robbing Norma and myself of a richer, fuller relationship. I just didn't realize it—until I heard a word picture intended for somebody else.

It's been many years and hundreds of counseling sessions since Jim came by the office. But I can still remember what was said that afternoon, and for good reason. Susan's word picture still has the same corrective effect on my marriage that it did the first time I heard it.

Setting the Stage

It was late on Sunday afternoon, and Jim was out in the shop off the garage. Besides watching sporting events, he had two hobbies but not much time to spend on either one. The first was dining out at nice restaurants, which he would do nightly if they didn't have to worry about paying off their charge-card bills. His other love was lying in pieces before him.

Like most young boys, Jim had gone through a model-building stage. He had just never gotten over it. Spread before him was his most ambitious project to date: a wooden model of a mid-1800s clipper ship, complete with slotted planks, three-foot masts, hand-tied rigging, and full sails yet to be cut.

With all the stress of teaching and coaching, Jim found that dining out and model building were two great ways to unwind. Knowing he was most open to talking while sitting at either a restaurant table or his hobby bench, Susan approached him in the shop.

"How's this one coming?" she said, secretly hoping this latest model wouldn't end up in their bedroom like so many others.

"Great!" he replied. "This will look perfect in the bedroom! I've got just the place picked out for it."

Wisely, she decided a discussion about which room would become a harbor for the clipper ship could wait until another time—and another word picture.

"Honey," she said, "I wanted you to know again how much I appreciated the story you told me a while back. It really made sense, and I'll try to be more encouraging."

"Are you kidding?" Jim said, looking up from his ship. "You've been great these past couple of weeks. I know you're really trying hard, and I appreciate it."

Compliments from her husband had been on the endangered species list for some time. His flattering words surprised her so much, they not only warmed her heart but also caused her to blush. They gave her more courage, too, to go on with the word picture she had been practicing all week with another coach's wife.

"Thanks, Honey. It means a lot that you can see I'm trying. You know I came from a pretty critical family, and it's easy for me to get that way with you.

"Jim, when you were telling your story, I not only understood it, but felt as if I *lived* it. All my life I wanted to be loved and hugged by my father when I came home, but all I ever got was anger or neglect. I don't want our home to be that way. I know I won't be perfect, but I promise I'll really work on what I say to you."

"That's great!" Jim said with a big smile, bending over his model ship and thinking word pictures were the greatest thing since chocolate ice cream.

"But Jim," Susan continued, "could I talk to you about something?"

"Sure, fire away."

"I'd like to share a word picture of my own that expresses how I'm feeling about our relationship."

Inside Jim's mind, a little alarm sounded. He glanced over at the portable phone, hoping it would ring to his rescue. He even glanced around for the boys, who were always doing something semi-destructive to the house or each other. Running after them had saved him from more than one serious conversation. But Susan had picked her time well.

Reluctantly, he shrugged his shoulders. "Sure," he said, leaning back on his bench, and fell into a life-changing word picture.

More Than Leftovers

Ignoring "that look" on Jim's face, Susan took a deep breath and began speaking. "Honey, you're a really hard worker. That's why you always stay up late grading papers, watching game films, or doing something else important. What that all means is that by the time you come to bed, you're worn out.

"Because you get so little sleep, you can barely get out of bed the next morning. But there's something that always succeeds in getting you into the shower and out the door, and that's your three-cheese omelet and a cup of coffee."

Jim had to smile. The deli, where all the varsity coaches met, served an outstanding breakfast.

"I'd like to tell you a story I made up about your day," she began. "After a few hours' sleep, you head off for breakfast and have the time of your life with the other coaches. You talk about some new trick play you're going to run in the next game; what the new school board superintendent will decide about overtime pay; or how much better the game was when you all were playing. Things like that."

It's all true so far, Jim had to admit.

"I'm not exactly sure what you order, but I bet you

have your favorite omelet, with sliced avocados on the side, accompanied by homemade, honey-wheat bread smothered with butter and preserves. Oh, and I almost forgot, you probably top it off with a tall glass of ice-cold milk and a small glass of fresh-squeezed orange juice. Am I pretty close?"

Susan was making educated guesses based on the hundreds of breakfasts she had seen him eat. She could see by his enthusiastic response that his mind was drifting back to his favorite breakfast place.

"When your meeting is over, you all slap each other on the back and then argue about who's paying the bill. But before you go out to the car, you do something different: You ask the man behind the counter for a paper sack. Then you return to the table, pick a few pieces of egg and toast from your plate, and drop them into the sack. You put the sack into your Nike tennis bag—the one you carry instead of a briefcase —and head off to school."

Until the part about the sack and crumbs, Jim had been right with her. Now his mind was racing to figure out what significance a paper sack could have in her word picture. However, before he could ask any questions, she went on.

"All morning you teach history, which you enjoy. And before you know it, it's time for lunch. Because your office is over in the field house, you and the other coaches go off campus to a nice coffee shop. There, you order a turkey tenderloin pie, its flaky, homemade crust filled with chunks of white meat, the freshest of vegetables, and a creamy white sauce. Of course, it wouldn't be lunch if you didn't have their fifty-item salad bar on the side and a huge glass of brewed ice tea.

"You all have a great time talking sports and telling jokes. Then, just as you did after breakfast, you ask for a small sack when you're finished. The waitress brings it to the table, you drop in little bits of leftovers, and then place it inside your Nike bag before heading back to school.

"After a long afternoon of teaching algebra, it's back to school for football practice. Afterward, it's late in the afternoon, and you've still got things to talk about, so you guys all drop by the ice-cream parlor next to the mall.

"You have a brief struggle with your calorie-counting conscience, but when the waitress comes, you order their chocolate tower sundae—the one with four scoops of premium ice cream and ladles of hot fudge and butterscotch toppings. On the side you get a small cup of crushed almonds and a diet Pepsi. Of course, you get the diet drink because it cancels out the calories in the ice cream," she said with a grin.

"Of course," Jim said, grinning back. That was one of his standard jokes when he bellied up to the ice cream trough.

"And for the third time, you gather up what's left on the table. You scrape off some whipped cream and toppings, and some of the melted ice cream and nuts. Then you dump it all into a sack and put it in your tennis bag."

Not only was Jim getting hungry listening to her story, but he was puzzled trying to figure out what she was getting at. *Why did I have to tell her how to create word pictures in the first place?* he grumbled to himself. Finally, he couldn't stand the suspense any longer.

"Are you trying to tell me I've got so many food stains on my old Nike bag that it's time to buy a new one?" Jim asked with a hopeful smile. "Or are you hinting that you want me to take you out for dinner tonight?"

It was a feeble attempt to speed things up or at least

break some of the tension building up inside him. Unfortunately, his smoke screen didn't work.

"Now, come on. Let me finish," Susan said. "I'm almost through. All day, while you've been at work, I've been wanting to have you near me. I think about getting to go somewhere together where we can sit and catch up on everything. But it's not just me. The boys love you so much, and want to be a part of your life, too.

"Well, after waiting for you all day, we finally hear the garage door open. We're so eager for you to spend time with us that we line up at the back door. Maybe you'll even take us out to a nice dinner where we can all talk and laugh and get to know each other better.

"And then the door opens, but you don't stop to talk to us or fill us in on the things that happened in your day. You just walk by and hand the boys and me a doggy bag each. And then you walk over and turn on the television set or come out here to your hobby bench. Instead of getting to enjoy a real meal together with you, we're left standing at the door, holding these soggy, smashed doggy bags.

"It's not that I don't want you to have a hobby, Jim. That's not why I'm telling you this. You need time to unwind and relax, and I want that for you. But all day, the kids and I have longed to be with you. We've waited to find out what's going on in your life—and for you to ask what's going on in ours. But you've already spent the day with people who are most important to you—your players and the other coaches. So instead of giving us your best when you come home, all we get are leftovers.

"I think that's the reason I've felt so cheated in our relationship over the years and why I've been so critical of you during football seasons. Growing up, I remember how my mother was always so hungry for meaningful communication with my dad. And now I'm standing at the door of my marriage, just as she did, waiting to enjoy a satisfying meal with you, hoping for time to talk and laugh and get to know you, longing to communicate the way you do every day with the guys. The boys and I all want that, but all we get are doggy bags. Honey, don't you see? We don't need leftovers. We need *you.*"

The last thing I had expected to run into that afternoon was a word picture, particularly one that stopped me dead in my tracks. When Jim finished telling it, he wasn't the only one with tears in his eyes. I knew I couldn't escape the message it carried for my life as well.

Because of my travels and all the hours spent helping other people, my schedule was probably twice as crowded as Jim's. Just like him, I was giving my wife and children table scraps on nights and weekends. Deep inside, I knew it. And Norma and the kids knew it.

That evening when I went home, things began to change around my house, as they had in Jim's. I told Norma the word picture I'd heard, and her response confirmed we had a problem. I had been handing out scraps to my family instead of a nourishing meal of emotional attachment.

In the weeks that followed, I couldn't walk in the door at night and head toward the television without realizing I was handing out little, brown bags. I hated to admit it, but my couch-potato days were numbered.

Something else also changed as a result of that word picture. I called my supervisor at the time, telling him I needed to cut back my travel. Having been deeply challenged to spend more quality time with my family, I was prepared to look for another job if my company couldn't change my job description. In particular, I would find a job that didn't rob my family of me.

Everyday objects, when tied to another person's interests, can supercharge communication with meaning.

Leftovers are just one of the thousands of everyday objects found in this second of four wells. Each of these objects, when tied to another person's interests, can supercharge communication with meaning.

They can also provide tremendous inner strength and encouragement, as another man found. For him, an everyday object conveyed hope to live in a hopeless situation. What's more, it gave his sons a lifelong respect for him and their country.

A Picture of Hope in a Pit of Despair

From the moment his landing craft ground to a halt, Jerry felt as if he had arrived at the very gates of hell. All around him was black, volcanic ash that stung his eyes and wouldn't brush off his skin. And the terrible sights and smells of death were everywhere.

Iwo Jima meant nothing to Jerry when he first heard the words. But time took care of that. Soon enough, as a nineteen-year-old in the Fifth Marine Division, he realized the two words meant every nightmare he ever had would come true before his eyes.

The landscape was pockmarked with craters as a massive flotilla of warships pounded the island in advance of the Marines' landing. However, the enemy had had nearly four months to choose its positions, so the nonstop bombardment generally had no effect.

With so much time to prepare for the American invasion, they had every inch of beach covered with rifle, machine gun, and artillery fire.[1]

Jerry's first hours on the beach were spent trying to dig a foxhole deep enough to escape the murderous fire raining down. However, the volcanic sand filled his hole as quickly as it was dug, leaving him exposed to the constant enemy fire. As the day became more hot and humid, Jerry threw off his poncho and field jacket. But the temperature dropped so radically after dark that he shivered all night in the cold.

It was a miracle, earned by blood and raw courage, that he and the other Marines ever fought their way off the beach. Nonetheless, their advance came at tremendous cost. Bodies from both sides lay torn and twisted beyond recognition, mute testimony to what was ahead.

While we talked with this veteran of three beach landings, his eyes filled with tears as he thought back to those horrible days. Time has dimmed some of the horrors he saw and heard, but five words a fellow Marine said to him are still as vivid as brilliant sunlight.

The date was February 21, 1945—two days after the landing. Jerry had taken cover in a small crater formed by an exploding artillery shell. The shelling from back in the mountains had kept everyone awake almost all night. The morning had dawned with falling rain and a restless fog drifting in the distant, higher slopes. But when the skies cleared and the Japanese could pick out their targets, the artillery bursts were joined by small-arms fire.

Jerry had already given up all hope of coming off the island alive. Of the fourteen men in his rifle section, only he and five others hadn't been wounded or killed. In just two days, he had already seen far too much death. But its cruel hand was just beginning to strike: More Marines would die on Iwo Jima than on all the other battlefields of World War II combined.[2] So many had died or been wounded around him already that he felt he had as much chance of living as keeping a soap bubble from bursting in the wind.

That's when his corporal crawled up next to him and flashed him a grin. "You still alive, Jerry?" he said in his Southern accent, offering Jerry a swig from a priceless canteen of water. "We're gaining on 'em, you know."

"How do you know that?" Jerry answered back with a thin smile. "Nobody came running up to me with a white flag last night."

"Look here, son, I have it on good authority. Tomorrow you'll see our boys on top of that hill. We're going to make it." Then he looked up at the fog-tipped volcano and spoke the words Jerry has never forgotten: "You'll see the flag tomorrow."

From the time the Marines first sighted Iwo Jima from the decks of their ships, they had been looking up at the highest point on the island. It was the top of Mount Suribachi, an extinct volcano. It was only 550 feet high, but the way death rained down from its steep, ragged slopes, it seemed more like Mount Everest. To have the American flag up there would mean that—at least from this hill—death would have lost its frightening foothold. It would also be the best sight any Marine had seen since he had landed.

As events turned out, Jerry wouldn't see the flag for another two days. And his corporal would never see it. He was killed in action that night. But on February 23, 1945, the hill was taken.

As the Stars and Stripes flew above them for the first time, men all over the island stood and cheered, ignoring the risk of exposing their position.

When Jerry saw the flag, the words his corporal had spoken came back in full force. And those same words would give him strength to carry on during the next eight days until he was critically wounded and carried off the island.

"When I got off Iwo alive, I felt my life had been given back to me," Jerry said. "You never forget something like that. In the years since, whenever I've had things go wrong I remember my corporal's words. When things look their toughest, I just think back and say to myself, 'Hang in there, Jerry. You'll see the flag tomorrow.'"

Over the years, in his times of deepest trial, Jerry remembered the words that always lifted his spirits. He often used them with his sons, too, as they grew up. He would tell them, "You'll see the flag tomorrow," if they lost an important game, failed an exam, or broke up with a girlfriend. The phrase was always said with his arm around his sons, and it always gave them new hope for another day.

Jerry has never discussed with his sons all the horrible details of his eleven days on Iwo Jima. But he has told them enough so that they carry around a piece of that forsaken island in their minds—the emotional word picture he took off "the rock." They remember five hopeful words that spoke of a better day ahead and offered the courage to wait for it.

In the late '60s, it became fashionable at many schools to burn American flags. But Jerry's sons, who were college students during that time, never would have considered such an act. The flag flew too proudly and stood too personally in their lives. It not only symbolized for them a proud country but it also was an intimate symbol of hope, courage, and endurance.

They couldn't look at a flag without seeing what was behind it. In fact, they still can't. The flag isn't just a pattern of stars and bars to them. It stands for their father who lived, and the many men who died, on battlefields such as Iwo Jima.

The Well of Everyday Objects

Using everyday objects to form a word picture (like a doggy bag, an American flag, a watch, a chair, and so forth) can make a vivid, lasting impression in your listener's heart.

Take a moment right now to reflect on your relationships. Is there someone you need to encourage who's facing a difficult time? A word picture can help. Is there someone who's getting further away from the family, and you want so much to bring him back? A word picture can help. The Well of Nature and the Well of Everyday Objects are two places to seek help or hope. You can also look for pictures in the third well, the Well of Imaginary Stories.

Read on to learn how the president of a company dramatically changes a pushy saleswoman.

CHAPTER NINE

The Well of Imaginary Stories

Sales had been strong for another quarter. Jay Campbell sat at his desk, smugly satisfied as he glanced at the glowing reports he had been handed that day. As the founder and president of his company, he'd seen it grow by leaps and bounds, particularly because of its relationship with one major firm that consistently ordered huge quantities of its products.

I may even take the afternoon off and try and get in some golf, he was thinking to himself when his secretary buzzed him.

"Excuse me, sir, but it's Mr. Devlin calling," she said. "I thought you'd want to know."

Less than an hour ago, in his firmest CEO voice, Jay had told his secretary to hang out the "I'm-in-a-meeting" sign. However, like all experienced executive secretaries, she knew certain names removed any sign posted on the door.

Mr. Devlin was the president of Valco, the major company responsible for most of those glowing sales.

So Jay's initial irritation at being interrupted was quickly replaced with his usual grudging respect for his secretary's wisdom.

Punching the button next to the flashing light, Jay picked up the receiver and said, "Hi, Mark. What are you doing this afternoon?"

"What am I *doing?*" The voice on the other end of the phone spat out the words. "I'll tell you what I'm doing. I'm trying to calm down after telling one of your saleswomen to get out of my office, and I'm not doing a very good job of it!"

"You had to do *what?*" Jay said, all five of his senses snapping instantly to attention. Pictures of plummeting sales figures exploded in his mind as the voice continued its red-hot tirade.

"This woman from *your* office took an hour of my office manager's time, trying to force her to place a new order. And that was after she'd already been told no. Then, when I came out and told her to leave because she was taking up so much office time, she told me I was *rude* for not listening to her pitch about a new product!

"Listen, Jay. I don't care how much money you could save us. When I tell somebody no, I mean no! And I'm telling you, if that woman ever comes back in our office again, you can cancel our current agreements and forget about our purchasing anything from you in the future."

Click! The phone on the other end of the line sounded like a door slamming.

Jay had been chewed out in his time. There had been his father's angry words when he had given his pet turtle a bubble bath, his football coach's screams when he fell asleep during the game films, his drill sergeant's four-letter blasts about everything he did. Even his wife could lay down the law at times. But to have his most important customer chew him out because of how one of his sales agents had acted—*that* was too much.

Fuming, Jay paced the office, thinking about the problem he had on his hands. Without hearing a name, he knew who had made the sales call. After all, there was only one woman on his sales force.

Sally was the most productive salesperson he had. The last four months she'd been the volume leader, hands down. She had great skill and determination in closing the sale. But lately she'd become so pushy that she closed as many doors as she opened. Jay liked her enthusiasm and hard-driving nature, and didn't want to fire her. But he realized he had come close to losing an account that was the lifeblood of his business. He knew he would have to confront her that very afternoon.

In preparation for the meeting, Jay turned to the Well of Imaginary Stories for help. After choosing the right word picture, based on one of the most embarrassing things he felt could ever happen, he mentally practiced it a few times and waited for Sally's return.

Sally didn't know it, but his words were about to grab her by the collar. In fact, his imaginary story would shake her world so forcefully that simply mentioning their conversation in the future would instantly cause her to back off from being too pushy.

"Come on in," Jay said when Sally peeked her head into his office. It was only on rare occasions that she was summoned into the president's office. This time his note on her desk had read "Urgent."

"I came as soon as I got your note, Mr. Campbell," Sally said. With relief, she noticed he was smiling as he rose from his chair.

"Please, come in and close the door. Take a chair over here," he said. "There's something I'd like to talk to you about." As she sat back, he launched into his word picture.

"Sally, when the company first started, I was the one doing all the sales calls. And during that time, do you know what I used to think would be the absolute worst thing imaginable?"

Jay didn't wait for an answer but went right on with his story. "Picture this. I'm in the boardroom of one of our top clients, all excited about making a presentation. I've got all my charts and graphs ready. Without a doubt, I'm 100 percent prepared to knock the ball out of the park and sign a contract on the spot.

"Well, the chairman of the corporation is sitting next to me. He says a few kind words of introduction, and then it's my turn to stand up and present our product to the entire board.

"I throw myself into the presentation. I'm talking loudly and gesturing like crazy when my hand suddenly hits the coffee pot in front of me, knocking it right into the president's lap! I'm talking about an entire pot of scalding coffee.

"You can imagine the scene. He's screaming and jumping up and down. Everyone else around the table is trying hard not to laugh, but you can tell people are cracking up on the inside. So I grab a handful of paper towels and try to help dry off the president. But because of where the coffee spilled, drying him off is pretty embarrassing in itself. Finally, thoroughly disgusted with me, he grabs the paper towels and tries to dry himself off.

"The whole time, I'm working to calm him down so I can salvage my sales presentation. I point to the charts and graphs I've worked on so long, showing how much money they'll save with this new product. But he's not interested in hearing about it anymore. He's having a difficult time sitting next to me, much less listening to me."

The picture her boss acted out while he was telling

the story was so comical that, in spite of herself, Sally was laughing right along with him.

There was a long pause after the laughter subsided. Sally finally asked, "Mr. Campbell, did you bring me in here just to tell me this story?"

"Well, in a way I did, Sally," he said, his voice and manner becoming serious.

"You see, this morning you poured scalding coffee right into someone's lap."

Another long silence stood between them before Sally looked down and said in a faltering voice, "What do you mean?"

Deep inside she knew what he was talking about, but she felt justified in working so hard to get that office manager to hear all of her presentation. After all, she had worked so hard in putting it together, and in her heart she felt the manager was wrong in not taking the time to listen.

"Sally, this morning when you were at the Valco office making your presentation, you were so excited you knocked a whole pot of scalding coffee into their business manager's lap.

"I know you do a great job of presenting our products. You also work hard at overcoming sales resistance. But for all your good intentions, you almost lost us our key client because you were far too pushy. Their business manager made it clear she wasn't interested in buying anything else at this time. Yet you still took an hour, trying to force her into a decision she couldn't make.

"To top it off, when the president came out and asked you to leave, you scalded him, too! In fact, telling him he was rude for not letting you finish was like opening the lid and just dumping hot coffee all over him. He called me to talk about it after you left."

Jay moved over next to her chair and looked her

right in the eye. "Sally, pouring scalding coffee on people will only ruin relationships and lose accounts that take years to establish—not get you a sale. And I must say that I'm concerned about you as an employee and as a person. You see, people talk, Sally. I know you're having trouble in relationships with the other sales reps. I know there's always competition and petty jealousy, and I'm not trying to take away any edge you might have. But you're ruining your relationships around the office by pouring coffee on people. And while I'm not trying to be too personal, I imagine you're probably doing it to your friends outside the office as well.

"If you scald people once, they may chalk it up to an accident. But if you keep doing it, you'll be the loneliest person in the world. If you want to sentence yourself to loneliness in your personal life, that's your decision. But if you keep scalding our key clients, it will cost you your job."

Others had tried to talk to Sally about her overaggressiveness—both at work and in her personal relationships—but she had always rationalized it away as jealousy. Every time she would excuse herself by saying, "They don't understand the situation" or "There's nothing wrong with having strong opinions."

Sally came from a family whose anger and fighting had become ingrained in her. Hearing "no" from a customer ignited all her old emotions, causing her to overreact and snap into her verbal attack mode. She had never been willing to look at her overly aggressive nature, because it would have forced her to look at too many painful memories at the same time.

For years, no one or nothing could crack her iron-clad defenses. But a significant conversation did—when her boss caught her broadside with an emotional word picture. It was as if he had ripped up a sixty-foot billboard from beside the freeway and planted it right in her front yard. This time, she couldn't miss the message that she was too pushy.

Jay was to tell us later, "Sally is still my top salesperson, and she's still pretty aggressive. Only now she's a lot more sensitive with our customers. In two years, to my knowledge, she hasn't scalded anybody else—including anybody at Valco."

This businessman didn't realize it, but he had not only saved Sally her job, he had also given her a tremendous gift. Her attitude had been revolutionized and redirected with her coworkers and friends.

Her boss's ultimatum, wrapped in a word picture, did more than scare her. It changed her. His clear picture grabbed her emotions so forcefully that she couldn't get overly aggressive with someone and not imagine herself holding a pot of scalding coffee.

Imaginary stories unlock the limitations that are often a part of everyday words.

In this third well, Jay tapped into a source of word pictures that is limited only by a person's imagination. In fact, imaginary stories unlock the limitations that are often a part of everyday words.

As we mentioned earlier, people love to listen to a story. When the tale begins, it's an open invitation for them to try to guess its outcome. It also locks in their attention and leaves a lasting memory of what we say.

Imaginary stories can use everyday objects or items from nature, as we've seen in the two previous wells. In addition, they can picture an event, a situation, or an occupation and thereby pull the listener into the scene.

Already, you have thousands of options for word

pictures available in these three inexhaustible wells. However, pictures from the fourth well may capture a person's heart more quickly than anything else.

In the Well of "Remember when . . ." you'll see how a word picture has been a tremendous help to the two of us as wc work together on books and conferences. "Remember when . . ." calls to mind something terribly embarrassing and instantly changes our attitudes and actions.

CHAPTER TEN

The Well of "Remember When . . ."

While each of the three wells we've looked at can maximize our communication, this fourth well has an important advantage over the others: the ability to draw on a picture already lodged in a person's memory. And by causing someone to remember a past event, we also trigger vivid feelings he or she experienced at that time.

In a recent study, doctors tried to find the areas of the brain that controlled memories.[1] Working with volunteers, the doctors electrically stimulated portions of the cortex and found their subjects would suddenly remember such things as a smell of something they'd eaten or a particularly enjoyable experience. After a while, the doctors noticed an unexpected side effect in the volunteers: When a certain memory was sparked, the *feelings* accompanying that earlier event were also recalled.

In a personal way, I (John) have seen this phenomenon with my father and other combat veterans. My father spoke to us in detail about his war experiences only one time. That was back in 1969, the day before my twin brother, Jeff, and I were facing the draft for the Vietnam War. For almost two hours, he told story after story of World War II. He did so because if we were drafted, he wanted us to know that war was not like the movies portrayed it.

Many veterans experience an unpleasant side effect to remembering the horrors of war. In recounting the graphic mental images, they once again feel the fear, anger, and hurt. No wonder they avoid talking about war. But what effect does this finding have on meaningful communication?

When you link a present message to a past experience or event, you take a direct path to a person's emotions, thereby multiplying the impact of your message.

When you link a present message to a past experience or event, you take a direct path to a person's emotions. That's because your words mix with past feelings, thereby multiplying the impact of your message. The end result is that the words you want to convey are electrified with incredible vividness and clarity.

As a rule, men are much less in touch with their emotions than women are. So as men face the task of unearthing past events and memories in the counseling process, they also face a flood of emotion. In large part, that's why so many men are initially resistant to seeking personal or marriage counseling. If they can overcome this threat, linking memories with feelings does have its positive side. That's especially true in the area of meaningful communication.

For example, let's say you've gone through a major

difficulty with someone. By using a word picture from the Well of "Remember When . . ." you can instantly tap into the emotions that were part of that experience. By drawing on them, you create an emotional bond that brings a deeper level of understanding to the conversation.

Do you need to straighten out a problem? To move deeper in a relationship? To clarify an important point in a conversation? To thank someone for a kindness? Then your memory of a past experience together can hold the key to finding and using an effective word picture.

Over the years, one especially graphic word picture drawn from the Well of "Remember When . . ." repeatedly has kept us on track at the office and has prevented us from making spur-of-the-moment decisions that could prove disastrous.

"Remember When We Were at Forest Home?"

If you're ever within earshot of our office, it won't be long until you hear one of us say, "Remember when we were at Forest Home?" When these words are tossed into the midst of a conversation or decision we're facing, they always bring new light—and more thought and reality—to the subject. This happens because the phrase represents a powerful word picture to us, stemming from one of the most embarrassing, humiliating moments of my (John's) life.

Located in the beautiful mountains of Southern California, Forest Home is one of the finest conference centers in the country.[2] Because of its incredible food, outstanding program, and the natural beauty surrounding the camp, it's jam-packed during the summer.

Several years ago, we were asked to bring our families and speak there. Since Gary was a veteran public speaker, he was asked to address the entire group of more than 450 people each morning. And I was asked to speak at an afternoon elective session—a tremendous honor because it would be my first time at Forest Home.

For months I worked to perfect my message. I'd been told to expect from forty to sixty people, and I came loaded with facts, files, and footnotes. Deep inside, I knew this would be a major step forward in my speaking career. Little did I know it would also be a banana peel upon which I would slip and fall face-first!

During Gary's first morning talk, he was illustrating a point about helping people accept and value each other's differences. In doing so, he explained that we often use an excellent personality test—called the Performax[3]—to help couples relate better together. That's when it happened.

In a moment of inspiration, he told everyone assembled, "This test can be so helpful in a marriage or a family that John can give it to all of you this afternoon. Instead of doing his regular elective, I'm certain he'll switch and give each of you the Performax!"

The idea sounded even better after he had said it aloud, so with more volume and intensity he continued, "That's right, folks. Dr. Trent is a qualified instructor in the test. A bona fide expert! I don't know what you've got planned for this afternoon. But whatever it is, cancel it. I guarantee you, the time you spend with John will be the most important hour of the entire week!"

I froze in my chair at the rear of the auditorium. My brain kept replaying his words. I couldn't believe my ears. Fear instantly gripped me. I wanted to jump up and yell, "Gary, wait a minute! What are you saying? I've prepared for months to do something else! Besides, there's no time to order the reams of tests and handouts I'd need for a group this size!"

As Gary continued to talk, I could tell what his motives were. Not only was he thinking that people would be greatly helped by going through this test, but he also was trying to drum up support for my afternoon elective and make me an instant Forest Home success!

Before I had the courage (or the intelligence) to jump up and say something, Gary closed his presentation with another moving appeal for every man and woman to attend my session. He laid it on so thick that anyone not attending my elective would have been labeled an introverted, psychopathic slug.

Though numb all the way to my toes, with a Herculean effort I stumbled forward to see if Gary had been stricken with mental illness. Perhaps that's what caused him to say what he did. On my way to the platform, mobs of people kept walking by, slapping me on the back and saying things such as, "Hey, I can't wait until your session!" and "Our family was going on the Jeep rides today, but we're canceling to hear you speak!" By the time I reached Gary, I'd already received ten times more positive feedback than I'd ever gotten for a message. And that was before I'd spoken my first word at Forest Home!

Like a presidential candidate sweeping up delegates in state after state, I was caught up in the tremendous momentum created by people's expectations. And when I finally talked to Gary, he got me even more pumped up.

"You can do it, John!" he said. "You don't need the actual test to hand out. Just explain what it says and wing it. I know it'll go great! Now goooo get 'emmmm, Big Guy!"

By the time Gary was finished with me, I was ready to sprint to the podium and lay it on them right then.

The hour and a half between lunchtime and my elective seemed like forever. I figured my presentation would change lives, restore marriages, and cure every parenting problem known to humanity.

I also envisioned the camp director coming up afterward. There I would be at the podium, trying to look humble as I basked in the thunderous applause of a second—no, third—spontaneous standing ovation. He would shake my hand, offering me a lifetime invitation to speak at Forest Home each summer as he led cheers for my talk.

As I waited for everyone to return from lunch, I paced back and forth, thinking about what I'd say when presented with my "Speaker of the Year" award. Instead, I should have been panic-stricken about the terrible trouble I was in. With Gary's communication skills and years of experience, he no doubt could have "winged it" that afternoon. And the people would have gone away feeling it was the best hour of their week. I made the mistake of thinking I could get the same result.

I'd prepared for months to entertain and instruct a small group in a classroom setting. But soon I stood watching in horror as more than 500 people crammed into the main auditorium. All but a handful of people had canceled their afternoon activities of horseback riding, golfing, family outings, or napping just to hear about a test that could change their lives.

Not only were all the Forest Home campers and staff there, but many people had also called their friends in nearby towns. Cars jammed the parking lot, from which rivers of people flowed toward the auditorium to hear this "incredibly important" session. Instead of an average-sized elective, I was speaking to one of the largest crowds of the summer!

Sitting in the front row were the camp director, staff, and my wife and daughter. Many in the packed meeting room had skipped lunch and been sitting for almost an hour to save seats for friends and family.

The excited chatter of the crowd was replaced by an expectant hush as I walked up to the podium and looked over the sea of faces. Like the anticipation for the opening snap of the Super Bowl or the first number of a singing legend's final concert, there was an air of electricity in the room—electricity that would soon turn into a massive shock. It was my once-in-a-lifetime opportunity to fulfill my destiny as a public speaker and stand where the "big time" speakers had stood before. But suddenly I realized I was in big trouble.

The hush that came over the crowd when I started my message quickly became a death-like silence. The harder I tried to explain what the test was like—*if we had it to pass out*—and what was in the packets—*if we'd been able to run them off*—I could sense the mood and facial expressions of the crowd changing from questioning . . . to disbelief . . . to shock . . . and finally to intense dislike.

All around the edges of the auditorium, people began getting up and walking out. A few even began stomping out from the front rows. For an hour, I was emotionally abused by the remaining sets of eyes. And I knew each pair of eyes had a mouth that would tell all its friends and family across the country that fun outdoor activities had been canceled to sit inside and be confused and bored by me. After more than an hour, I finally finished my explanation of the test and told everyone they were free to go—unless, of course, there were any questions.

Agreeing to speak on this subject without being prepared was my first big mistake. My second was that I shouldn't have bothered asking for questions. The only question asked was why the camp director ever invited me to speak. As people stormed from the building, they looked at me the way people of Paris looked at the Nazi scum who had held their city captive for years.

As soon as I stopped, I knew I had finished more than my talk. I was finished at Forest Home. More than that, I was finished everywhere else in the free world. After news of this fiasco got around, I couldn't get an invitation to speak at a Toastmaster's Club even if I held them at gunpoint!

My wife put on her bravest, most supportive, wifely smile. But she was the only one smiling. If I'd been living in the Old West, I no doubt would have been torn from her arms and hung from a limb of the closest tree.

As I headed back to our cabin to pack my bags, I prayed the earth would open up and swallow me in one giant gulp. Then I suddenly remembered something that multiplied my misery.

This was only the first day of camp!

I *couldn't* pack and leave. Dinner was in an hour and a half, and I'd have to walk in and face everyone!

And then there was tomorrow's elective!

Words cannot describe the feelings of embarrassment and humiliation that fell on me like a two-ton weight. I could imagine the cutting words and snide remarks people would make—or at least think— during the rest of the week.

Waiting for the camp to end made the time between December 26 and the next Christmas seem like a heartbeat. Instead of the forty to sixty people who normally would have attended my elective the rest of the week, I spoke to row upon row of empty seats. The few people who did come were my loving wife, my daughter who was too young to object, and a few women in Mother Teresa's range of sympathy and compassion.

The week finally ended, and our car crawled out of

the parking lot and inched back to Phoenix. Deep inside, I felt that what the atomic bomb had done to Hiroshima, my elective at Forest Home had done to my speaking career.

Several years have passed since that day of infamy in Southern California. Surprisingly, there were several positive results. First, Forest Home must have continued an active cover-up campaign, because invitations to speak haven't stopped coming in.[4] In addition, Gary felt so bad about what happened that we had several long talks that further strengthened our personal and working relationship. The discussions made me realize that the afternoon of agony was equally my fault. I should have put down my foot and explained my feelings. We also acknowledged that we're both capable of doing the same kinds of things to each other.

In addition, I learned a tremendous lesson about optimism versus reality. There are some hills so steep that the little train huffing "I think I can, I think I can, I think I can" had better realize it *can't,* pack its bags, and take the bus.

Finally, both Gary and I have gained one other major benefit through that experience. Years passed before I was invited back to Forest Home, but nearly every week we have used the phrase, "Remember when we were at Forest Home." It's our way of reminding each other that we should never again do something if we're not prepared to do an excellent job. It means "Slow down," "We don't have all the facts," "Maybe we're being unrealistic or too optimistic," or "We need to think this through before saying yes."

This one word picture says all these things and more. Because we've been drawn back to the memory of an event we shared together, the feelings return as well. And the mixture of words and feelings brings instant impact to our conversations. These benefits are ours—all because we've drawn time and again from the Well of "Remember When. . . ."

In the previous chapters, we've seen how powerful word pictures can be, how they're created, and the four wells from which to draw them. Nonetheless, some may say, "These are all great stories. But I'm still not exactly clear on how to personally use a word picture with my spouse or children."

As you turn the next page, you'll be stepping onto a bridge supported by five major pillars. These five pillars are what we feel support a successful and fulfilling marriage. We'll now look specifically at how a husband or wife can personally apply word pictures within a marriage to build intimacy as well as to span major and minor differences.

HOW CAN
WORD PICTURES
HELP MY MARRIAGE AND FAMILY LIFE?

CHAPTER ELEVEN

Pillars That Support a Fulfilling Marriage

PART ONE

A few years ago, we caught a plane to speak at a conference in southern Missouri. We'd heard on the news that high winds and torrential rains had been pelting the northern part of the state for several days. However, it never dawned on us that on the way to our destination—miles farther south—we'd come face to face with the dangerous aftermath of the storm.

We landed in the late afternoon in clear weather, then caught the shuttle bus to pick up our rental car. Aside from a few scattered clouds, it looked as if we had picked an ideal, early spring evening to drive the final leg of our trip. Heading out, we predicted the drive would take two hours.

The storm that had lashed out in fury north of us, however, left widespread havoc and danger in its wake. Fields had been turned into small lakes and were dumping their unwanted burdens into already swollen streams. Soon, every major tributary and river was choking from days of rain and mud—and roaring downstream toward a bridge we would soon have to cross!

The last rays of sunlight were fading to darkness when we came up over a hill and looked down on a small bridge less than a half-mile away. Suddenly, the brake lights of the car ahead of us flashed a brilliant red. The vehicle fishtailed as the driver wrestled it to a stop.

We quickly slowed and edged up to where his car had come to rest sideways in the road. That's when we saw what we had nearly driven over. Ahead of us, the raging waters were too much for one of the supports of the bridge. Several pillars had carried the bridge's weight for years. But in the past hour, the center support had shifted, causing the entire bridge to sag at a reckless angle.

We got out and looked at what had once been a calm, backwoods river, realizing how close we'd come to calamity. For the man ahead of us, a few yards were all that separated him from plunging into the debris-choked waters. Had he not stopped, he and his car would have certainly been swallowed.

In a dramatic way, we learned a lesson about bridge building that night. That is, a bridge is only as strong as the pillars that support it. And what's true of a bridge is also true of a marriage.

Building a Bridge of Intimacy That Won't Wash Away

We've counseled hundreds of couples over the years. In all our interviews, we have yet to meet one husband or wife who, when first married, didn't want to build a strong bridge of intimacy. However, after a few years many husbands and wives stand alone, stranded—one on one side of a problem-clogged river, the other on the opposite bank. Between them is their dying dream of intimacy—crumbling, twisting, and falling into a flood of bitterness.

Would you like to avoid that kind of anguish in your marriage? Would you like to build a solid support of meaningful communication that can withstand whatever storms may come? We've seen that intimate, fulfilling marriages have at least five major pillars of support. If they are driven deep and encased in the cement of unconditional commitment, these pillars can weather any trial or disappointment. But if any one of the five begins to crumble, the entire bridge that carries the marriage's dreams can sag dangerously.

A marriage built on the pillar of security can best withstand the inevitable storms of life.

Security: a Warm Blanket of Love . . . and the Best Birthday Present of All

The first structural support for a meaningful relationship is found in one word: security. A marriage built on the pillar of security can best withstand the inevitable storms of life. Conversely, insecurity can do major damage to a marriage, causing its entire structure to shake and crumble.

What do we mean by *security?* For us, security is the assurance that someone is committed to love and value us for a lifetime. It's a constant awareness that whatever difficulties we face, we'll work to solve our problems together. Security means we're fully committed to the truth and we'll be truly open to correction.

In our marriage book, *If Only He Knew,* we write

about how love, at its roots, is a decision—not a feeling. In that regard, one of the most loving things any spouse can do is decide to build security into his or her marriage.

To discover how word pictures can help meet that goal, let's examine a special gift that a woman named Charlotte gave her husband. For years, she had seen doubts and unreasonable fears smash against the pillar of security in their relationship. Yet in five minutes, she finally sent those feelings of insecurity downstream.

Putting Insecurity out the Door

Alan, Charlotte's husband, had been married once before. Back in high school, he fell head-over-heels for his wife-to-be and never lost that feeling until her untimely death at age thirty-two. For nine years afterward he felt like a shell—until one spring day when he met Charlotte, a cute, petite blonde with bright eyes and an energetic manner. Her constant smile and radiant personality made him feel ten years younger. For him, the relationship uncovered forgotten hopes, unearthed hidden feelings of love, and rooted out his deep loneliness.

After a lengthy courtship, they were married in Charlotte's home church. Alan tried his best to be an encourager and a loving support to his wife. He was patient when she was overly excited, consistently praised her for large and small accomplishments, and cared enough to point out areas where she needed to grow. He even helped her pursue a lifelong dream—to take a sabbatical from full-time work and get her college degree. He did this by moonlighting to pick up the economic slack. Not only did his after-hours efforts enable her to study without financial worry, but they also paved the way for the words "high honors" to appear on her diploma that hung in the hall.

In many ways, Alan was a model husband. Yet, try as he might, he never felt totally secure in their relationship. He didn't struggle with a lack of commitment, because he had vowed to love her for life. For her part, Charlotte had never given him the slightest reason to doubt her faithfulness. She consistently went out of her way to express her love and commitment.

Nonetheless, deep in his heart Alan carried a great fear. After losing his first wife to cancer, he was frightened the same thing would happen to Charlotte. And since she had a bright, perky personality and was ten years his junior, he felt sure she would leave him one day for a younger, more handsome, *college-educated* man.

Every time he walked down the hall of their home, he couldn't help thinking how her crisp, framed diploma made his old, faded trade-school certificate look small and cheap. And try as he might, he couldn't help feeling that one day his fears would become a reality. He would have only old pictures and a new layer of emotional pain to compound the nine years of past hurt.

Like a splinter pushed deep beneath the surface, his nagging insecurity remained a constant emotional irritant—until his fiftieth birthday. It was then that his wife gave him the gift of an emotional word picture that caused his doubts and fears to melt away in moments.

In the weeks leading up to his birthday, Alan avoided any mention of that day of infamy. He had turned forty without the usual traumatic thoughts. But fifty? Could he really be that old?

When the dreaded day finally came, part of him was

glad Charlotte didn't say anything about his birthday before he left for work. The other side poked at him with long fingers of insecurity, trying to scratch and pry at his tender spots of fear and doubt.

Of course she didn't say anything about your birthday this morning, the inner voice would whisper. *She's as embarrassed as you are about your age. Can't you see that? What do you really have to offer her now that you're* fifty?

These thoughts caused Alan to stay late at the shop that day. And when he finally punched out, the same feelings slowed his steps to his car and made him take the long way home.

Even driving slowly, he beat Charlotte home from work—as usual. Things looked as they always did when he pulled into the driveway. The paper boy had missed his usual three-point attempt to hit the front porch, and a stash of letters begged to be taken into the house. And as certain as sunrise and sunset, his aging retriever, Casey, stood on the porch. He wiggled with excitement and wagged his tail as if trying to shake it off.

Alan loved that dog. Casey was his last living link to the years of happiness with his first wife. Through the many dark days after she had died, when he'd sit each night on the back porch and cry, his silent, brown-eyed friend would nuzzle up next to him. Alan was sure the dog could sense his pain, and Casey's warm presence was a tremendous comfort to his broken heart.

On his way inside, Alan stopped a moment to pat Casey's head and watch his dog smile in ecstasy as he scratched beneath his chin. Then, after retrieving the mail and paper, he opened the door and reached for the light. But before his hand could flick the switch, another light flashed on and a host of his family and friends jumped from their hiding places.

"Surprise!" they shouted. "It's about time you got here!"

That evening, there was much kidding and fun, yet it was a sensitive time as well. For each person also wrote a tribute to Alan, testifying how his loving spirit had touched his or her life over the years. But Alan told us later that Charlotte gave him the greatest present of all—a gift that helped not only to dissolve the unfounded fears and insecurity in his marriage but also to replace them with a rock-solid trust.

It started when she gestured for everyone to give her their attention. "It's my turn to give Alan his present," Charlotte said. "And it comes in two parts."

First, she handed him a box containing a new watch. There were applause and oohs and ahs all around as he held up his new timepiece.

"It's something I know you've been needing. And whenever you look at it, I want you to think about me," she said, with a twinkle in her eye. "But I have another gift for you—a little story I'd like to tell while our friends and family are here.

"I've never told most of you about my background, but I guess I've always been like a hyper, cocker spaniel puppy—one that's always bouncing around and getting into something it shouldn't," she began.

There were nods and smiles of understanding all around the room. Everyone present knew that even on an off day, she was a nonstop whirlwind of activity. Basically, everyone thought of Charlotte as a party waiting to happen.

"But I grew up in a home where being a cocker spaniel wasn't acceptable. I always was disliked for being me and was made to feel I should have been something different. I was never brushed or combed, and every time I'd jump up for some attention or get into something I shouldn't have, I'd be knocked down and put on a choke-chain leash.

"I'm not going to go into it all, but by the time I was in high school, things got really bad. At one point, I was told I was a mongrel who'd never be worth anything. I was even put in a car and driven down to the local animal shelter and thrown out on its doorstep.

"I ran away before the people in the pound could grab me. But for years after that experience, I wandered around the streets, never really believing anyone could love me just as I was, a cocker spaniel.

"But then one day, Alan saw me walking by—matted hair and all—and he gently picked me up. I don't know how, but he believed that a purebred was beneath all that dirty, matted hair. And then he took me home, washed and brushed my coat, and even gave me a beautiful ribbon to wear.

"All my life, I'd been made to feel I was a mutt. But when I could see how much he believed in me and cared for me, I began to think I might have a pedigree after all."

Charlotte paused for just a moment to push back her hair. A quick glance around the room indicated she had everyone's attention—especially Alan's.

"Over these past six years, I've been loved and protected. I've even found that I have a lifetime friend to live with. There are days when the puppy in me still comes out, and I run around and accidentally knock things over. Even then, I'm still loved, not beaten and thrown outside," she said, turning toward Alan with her eyes dampened.

"After years of feeling like a mixed breed, I finally have a home where someone feels I'm a purebred champion. I finally have somewhere to go where I don't have to worry about changing and being something or somebody I'm not.

"Alan, I know you're the one with the birthday and presents, but I feel I've gotten the greatest gift of all.

That's because every day, I get to live with a man who says to me in a thousand different ways, 'I will never, ever take you away or put you back on the street again.' Honey, I love you with all my heart."

Charlotte had spent less than an hour thinking up and practicing her word picture, drawn from the Well of Nature. She knew Alan loved animals, especially Casey. She had originally thought her story would be just another way of adding a special touch to a surprise party. But it meant much more to Alan. It touched him so deeply that six years of insecurity and unfounded fear were swept away.

When it comes to building a bridge of intimacy in your marriage, is your own pillar of security solid? If you were to question your spouse—without any pressure or nonverbal threats—about how secure he or she feels in your relationship, what would the answer be?

Why not ask your spouse to choose, on a one-to-ten scale, how secure your actions and attitudes make him or her feel? If "one" equals total insecurity and "ten" is complete security, how high would you score? Have you ever asked your spouse what it would take during the next six weeks to move closer to complete security or what you could do to maintain it if you've already achieved that goal?

A bridge between husband and wife can't stand up to raging waters if the pillar of security is made of sandstone. By using word pictures to strengthen the self-esteem of your spouse, you not only will help him or her discover new levels of confidence, but you'll shore up your marriage with pillars of granite as well.

Of course, we realize it takes more than this language of love to build security in a marriage. Word pictures must also be linked with everyday actions that promote trust, truthfulness, and confidence. Other books we've written, including *For Better or Best, The Blessing, The Gift of Honor, If Only He Knew,* and *The Key to Your Child's Heart,* offer detailed instruction on developing specific traits that instill lasting security in a relationship.[1] If these nuts-and-bolts skills are lacking in your marriage, these books will serve as how-to manuals for your rebuilding effort.

Nonetheless, though actions may speak louder than words, the latter are still critical to a healthy marriage. Simply put, our spouses need to *hear* they're appreciated and *told* they're loved. Of all the ways to express praise and support, word pictures are the best, for they immovably plant words of security in a person's heart. And remember, they can build security in more ways than one.

In Alan's case, his wife used the language of love to praise him, and her expression of encouragement worked beyond her wildest dreams. In several previous examples, we've also seen that correction can be accomplished most effectively with an emotional word picture.

Remember Jim and Susan, each of whom told a story that brought the other to tears?[2] While tears shed over angry or insensitive words can erode security in a marriage, they can also act like glue to bond love and commitment.

Some of us need to stop right now and closely examine our everyday actions. We need to take an objective look at how well we're doing at building up or breaking down security in our marriage. This examination may prompt us to get more knowledge and skill with which to build security, or it may steer us toward a marriage-enrichment visit with a pastor or other counselor.

Once we've worked to establish this first pillar, we need to examine the second major support needed to hold up a healthy marriage. It involves something for which word pictures are custom-made: meaningful communication.

Meaningful Communication: Talking Heart to Heart

The word "communication" is derived from the Latin *communis,* from which we get "common."[3] Expressed another way, if a husband and wife are ever to communicate effectively, they must find common ground that spans their differences.

In chapter 4, we discovered enough natural differences between the sexes to choke a horse—or a marriage. Yet we also found that one of the most effective ways to bridge these differences is emotional word pictures. For this and all the other reasons we've given earlier, we should use word pictures in communication to:

- increase the clarity and vividness of our conversations
- rivet a person's attention
- capture someone's emotions
- cause others to remember our words
- replace black-and-white conversation with living color—and much more.

Word pictures are essential to creating intimacy and resolving conflict. Only by mastering this language of love can you achieve clear and powerful speech.

Security and meaningful communication are inescapable necessities if a bridge of intimacy is to last. In the following chapter, we'll examine the remaining three pillars that support a meaningful relationship. Set deep in the soil of your marriage, they'll carry years of weight without calamity.

CHAPTER TWELVE

Pillars That Support
a Fulfilling Marriage

PART TWO

To help span more of the inevitable differences
and disagreements over a marital life cycle, three
additional pillars are necessary. In the most
successful marriages we've seen, each couple has decided to keep an important flame alive—a flame that
can be ignited and fanned by an emotional word
picture.

Emotional/Romantic Times: Creating Moods That Bond

Keeping the flames of romance burning may not
seem as important to a relationship as security or
meaningful communication, but it is. This third pillar
can help stabilize a home, particularly through difficult times.

We're not implying that a couple must spend each
weekend night over a candlelight dinner. (In many
homes, the kids would have blown out, squirted out,
or eaten the candles long before the meal was finished!) But we are saying that wise couples never lose

sight of the importance of romance to their marital well-being. Take Rick, for example.

When he was old enough to date, his mother pulled him aside and explained the importance of romance. After having seen a lifetime of sensitive things his father had done for his mother—and the payoff in the close relationship they enjoyed—he took her advice.

In high school, he went the extra mile to open the car door and get corsages for special occasions. He made a point of remembering birthdays in a big way and sending cards for special accomplishments. After graduation, when he looked into the deep blue eyes of a girl in his freshman English class, he knew his practice was about to pay off.

During the four years of dating that followed, his constant stream of notes, cards, flowers, and creative dates with Nancy were a romantic introduction to a lifetime of love. When it came time to propose in their final year of college, he did so in an unexpected way.

He was accompanying Nancy to her parents' home for Christmas break. He realized she was beginning to expect he might pop the question any time, but he had other plans.

He had picked up her engagement ring the day before their departure and was bubbling with excitement as they checked in at the airline ticket counter. But then he froze in fear as they neared the security gates. He knew the ring in his pocket would set off the metal detector. The screaming alarm would force him to empty his pockets, and all his planning would be in vain.

Fortunately, the metal detector kept his secret, and they made their way to the departure gate. But even after boarding, Rick remained as nervous as an expectant father. Almost as soon as he sat down, he excused himself to go to the lavatory. But in reality, he went back to the galley. Trembling all over, Rick stepped up to the closest flight attendant and awkwardly pushed a black jewelry box into her hands. But he was so nervous that she became frightened and tossed it right back! Finally, after assuring her it wasn't an explosive, he talked her into serving Nancy a plate with her engagement ring on it instead of dinner.

Each of the flight attendants did a tremendous job of keeping the secret. Not once did they give Nancy any special attention that might have aroused her suspicions. They went about their duties, getting all the passengers seated, and after takeoff they came slowly down the aisle serving the meal.

Nancy occupied the middle seat between an elderly woman at the window and Rick on the aisle. The flight attendant served the older woman first, then Rick, and then there was a long pause. When Nancy finally realized something was wrong and looked up, she saw the entire crew surrounding her. Grinning from ear to ear, they placed a handmade, aluminum foil basket in front of her. Inside was the small jewelry case, which she opened with a cry of surprise.

"Yes, I'll marry you!" Nancy said, beaming as she hugged Rick. The elderly woman, along with all the crew, cheered. And then suddenly the intercom crackled to life as the captain congratulated Rick and Nancy and invited everybody on the flight to their wedding! The entire plane burst into spontaneous applause and laughter, and Nancy cried and laughed at the same time.

Whenever the story was told in years to come about how they got engaged in midair, Rick would chuckle and say their relationship had been downhill ever since. As the years passed, however, their marriage grew stronger. In fact, it was equaled only by the success Rick enjoyed in the oil business. During those years when his business flourished, he continued to go to great lengths to keep a spark of romance alive.

He would arrange for baby-sitters and would "kidnap" his wife for special dates. Or he would take a teddy bear with an "I love you" note taped to it, wrap it in aluminum foil, and stick it way back in the freezer alongside the foil-wrapped leftovers and meats. Sometimes it took months, but sooner or later Nancy would dig back into the freezer, looking for something to defrost for a meal. But instead of finding a chicken or roast, she'd find a frozen teddy bear with her husband's love note.

To many of their neighbors, they were a model couple that put Ken and Barbie to shame. Then, in a state where oil prices never dipped, the market crashed virtually overnight. Over the course of almost twenty-five years, Rick had accumulated a fortune. But in less then twenty-four months, he saw the fruit of his labors slip away to creditors and foreclosures.

Things got so desperate at one point that Rick had to do the unthinkable—something he never dreamed could happen. To make the monthly payment on their house, he had to sell her diamond engagement ring for needed cash.

Rick was finally forced out of the oil business altogether. They lost everything they had. For the first time since their marriage, he wasn't the joker he had always been. With so much pressure and pain because of the loss of his business, his endearing acts of romance dwindled to a trickle.

But when things looked the worst, Rick landed a promising job in another industry. Slowly, the family's outlook began turning around as his new company recognized and appreciated his business skills. But it wasn't until nearly two years later, when Rick and Nancy were out at dinner celebrating a new promotion at work, that she saw the Rick of old again. What he did that night was so romantic and meaningful that she was soon flying higher than the 36,000 feet where their commitment began.

"Nancy," Rick said as they looked out the window of the restaurant at the twinkling city lights far below, "don't you think the lights look like diamonds tonight?"

She nodded and smiled. "It's good to be back."

When he had been in the oil business, they had frequented this same downtown, high-rise restaurant. They had even hosted an anniversary party here for his parents several years before, treating over eighty people to a sumptuous meal. But that was years ago, and this was the first time they had been back since losing their business.

Nancy drank in the view from their perch high above the city. Indeed, the lights did dance below like glittering diamonds.

Just then the waiter arrived with their main course. He and his helpers had been just as attentive as in years gone by. She enjoyed watching their skills. They were always nearby to fill a glass or take away a dish, but never so close that they intruded on a conversation.

She had ordered her favorite dish, and it was set before her just as she remembered it—covered by the bright, silver warming dome that the waiter would whisk away with a flourish. Only this time, when he lifted the silver cover to expose her meal, all that was on her plate was a small, black jewelry box.

It took time for her mind to take in what was before her. After all, it had been almost twenty-five years since their engagement. Almost afraid to touch the box, she slowly reached out and carefully opened it. The engagement ring she had received years before was a beautiful, one-carat diamond. Now she was staring at a magnificent, two-carat stone, surrounded by a host of miniature diamonds.

Rick took his wife's hand in his own. "Nancy," he said, his voice filled with emotion, "you are like this diamond—beautiful, exquisite, precious. There are many facets about you that I love—your warmth, your faithfulness, your kindness. In each situation we encounter together, one of your facets catches a ray of light and sends back a splash of color to me. Even during the hardest of times, you look for the light, the good, the encouraging thing to do or say, and you take that light and reflect it to me in beautiful rainbows. You are the most priceless treasure God ever gave to me.

"The happiest day of my life was when I gave you your first diamond. The darkest day was when I had to ask for it back. Every time you look at this new diamond, I want you to remember that it represents the way I feel about you. Happy anniversary, Sweetheart—a little early."

It was almost eight months until their next anniversary, so his present definitely came as a surprise. Once again, a roomful of strangers were told they had just been "engaged," and broke into spontaneous applause. But just when Nancy reached the height of her emotions, she was hurled back to earth by the reality of the price tag.

"Rick," she said shakily, as if waking from a dream. "I'm so touched, but . . . where did you get the money?"

"I knew you'd ask that," he said with a wink. "I sold one of the kids."

"Seriously, I want to know," she said, a hint of fear creeping into her voice. Even though there were no longer wolves at the door, she knew they could ill afford to go into debt for a ring, especially one so beautiful.

"Well, I got the money from my dad."

"You did *what?*"

Throughout their darkest financial times, Rick had never turned to his father for help. His dad had been a successful businessman and would have given them everything he had. But Rick preferred to find his own way through their problems and so he had refused his dad's help.

"You know the gun set I get when Dad dies—the one he never uses? Well, we had a long talk a few weeks ago, and since neither of us hunts anymore, I cashed it in for the ring. Pretty good swap, don't you think?"

Rick's father had been an avid hunter and had a shotgun collection worth several thousand dollars. It was a personal treasure he planned to pass down to his son. In her mind's eye, Nancy could see the two grown men acting like children, plotting to get her this ring. Rick had come by his practical joking and romantic bent naturally—inherited straight from his father.

Knowing they had both given up something precious to buy the ring was almost too much for her to take. She kept staring at the diamond, knowing it stood for a love far beyond the price it would command in any jewelry store.

Rick's words penetrated straight to Nancy's heart because he used both an object as well as a verbal picture to communicate his love for her. His words, together with the visual symbol of his love, created a lasting image in Nancy's mind. Each time she watched the rainbow colors sparkle in her diamond, she heard Rick's affirming words, and they warmed her anew, creating confidence and strength in their marriage. The ring and Rick's words would always be a priceless reminder of how much he valued her, and of the special way he built romantic times and thoughts into their marriage.

* * *

Of course, most of us don't have a gun collection to swap for a diamond that could spark a romantic evening. But there's a priceless treasure we can give our spouses for only the cost of the air we breathe. It's available merely by drawing an emotional word picture from one of the four wells. For when it comes to generating romance in a relationship, men and women have seen their words turn to gold for centuries.

For example, consider King Solomon and his bride. Listen to the word pictures he used to capture her heart:

> Your eyes behind your veil are doves . . .
> Your lips are like a scarlet ribbon . . .
> Your temples . . . are like the halves of a pomegranate.[1]

She offers him a word picture with language of love all her own, saying of her fiancé:

> Like an apple tree among the trees of the forest,
> is my lover among the young men.
> I delight to sit in his shade,
> and his fruit is sweet to my taste.[2]

Or listen to Romeo and Juliet, creations of William Shakespeare. Their words of love—again captured in word pictures—have been immortalized for generations. Romeo says:

> But soft, what light through yonder window breaks?
> It is the East, and Juliet is the sun.[3]

> See how she leans her cheek upon her hand.
> O, that I were a glove upon that hand,
> That I might touch that cheek![4]

Or consider Juliet's bittersweet picture of her love for Romeo—a love she felt would last beyond his death:

> Give me my Romeo, and when I shall die
> Take him and cut him out in little stars,
> And he will make the face of heaven so fine
> That all the world will be in love with night
> And pay no worship to the garish sun![5]

In one of the most romantic relationships of modern times, Elizabeth Barrett Browning and her husband, Robert Browning, sent word picture after word picture to each other. A perfect example of hers begins with the oft-quoted words, "How do I love thee? Let me count the ways."[6]

Instead of counting all the ways, we know what some of you—particularly males—may be thinking: *Wait a minute! That's poetry! Do you mean to say I've got to make my word picture rhyme to build romance into my marriage? That's going too far!*

If we were saying that, not one man in a hundred would pick up this book or devise a word picture. Remember, poetry and fine arts come more from the heart than from the head. So we're not asking the typical fact-oriented male to become a Shakespeare to build romance in his marriage.

The greatest lovers of all time were those who used word pictures to win their mates.

However, the point is still valid. The greatest lovers of all time were those who used word pictures to win their mates.[7] So whether you use a word picture like Rick's—with straightforward, everyday speech—or a poem like Shakespeare's, in either case you're crafting lasting bonds of love.

Remember, if Solomon was wise enough to realize that a woman gains love and security through romantic words, so should we. Security, meaningful communication, and emotional/romantic bonding—all three provide strong support for an intimate relationship, and all three are best accomplished with the language of love.

In addition to the three pillars we've looked at, there are two more. Both can help support a bridge of intimacy that can take a couple safely above the rough, dangerous waters of inconsistency and emotional distance.

Meaningful Touch: the Silent Language of Love

Study after study has reached the same conclusion. An essential part of an intimate marriage is found right at our fingertips. Among many others, UCLA researchers have concluded that meaningful touch is crucial to the formation and preservation of an intimate relationship. In fact, research has shown that a woman, in particular, needs eight to ten meaningful touches each day just to maintain physical and emotional health.[8]

But many women's needs are unmet. The result is that outside the bedroom, a woman must often look to her children, relatives, or supportive friends to make up for a lack of meaningful touch from her husband.

Many husbands don't understand that by depriving a woman of nonsexual touching, they are opening the door for another man to provide that missing fulfillment.[9] That door never needs to be left open. Men need to realize that more than 80 percent of a woman's desire for meaningful touch is nonsexual.[10]

For example, holding hands while waiting in line,

giving an unrequested back rub for a few moments, gently stroking her hair (in the right direction!), and hugging her tenderly are all ways to build intimacy in a relationship.

Consistent, gentle touching is one of the most powerful ways to increase feelings of security, prime the pump for meaningful communication, and set the stage for emotionally bonding and romantic times. But what does meaningful touch have to do with word pictures? A great deal. A gentle hug, for example, can be one of the most powerful *nonverbal word pictures* of love.

Communication studies show that nonverbal messages are actually more powerful than verbal ones![11] Because of the incredible emotional weight of meaningful touching, the nonverbal picture of a hug left in a person's mind can solidify a relationship—just as it did for a man who called us one day on a radio talk show and told his remarkable story.

We were on one of our favorite radio call-in programs in Southern California. With his sensitive style, the host asked us to explain a relationship principle and would then encourage listeners to call with their problems, questions, or comments.

We had just finished explaining the significance of meaningful touch when a man we'll call George phoned us.

"When I was fifty-one years old, I suffered a major heart attack," he said. "I was rushed to the hospital, and because the attack was so severe, my wife called my father to come to my bedside.

"To my knowledge, my dad never told me he loved me. Nor did he ever say he was proud of me. He was always there and always supportive in his quiet way, but I still left home questioning whether he really loved and cared for me.

"But as I lay in that hospital bed, with the doctors telling me I might not make it, my seventy-year-old father was flying across the country to be at my side. He arrived the day after my heart attack, and when he came into my room, he did something I'll never, ever forget. He pulled up a chair next to my bed, sat down, and then took my hand in his. I couldn't remember him ever hugging or kissing me, but as I lay there in intensive care, with tubes running everywhere, he stayed for several hours, much of that time just holding my hand."

Up to that point, we thought we were hearing just another dramatic example of the powerful, symbolic picture that meaningful touch can leave behind. We weren't expecting what he said next.

"It still hurts to a degree that my father never said he loved me. But by reaching out and holding my hand, he expressed what he could never put into words. And it was just what I needed to know, because two days after he flew out to be at my bedside, he died of a stroke."

We adjusted our headphones to make sure we'd heard him correctly.

"I was the one expected to die, but I recovered and my father died," he said. "But when he came to my hospital room, he left me something for which I'll always be thankful. When he held my hand, he shouted the words he could never speak—words of love that I saw in his eyes and felt through his hands."

By definition, a word picture involves actual *words.*[12] But for this man, his father's touch spoke volumes and left behind a dramatic image of love and acceptance. And that word picture healed years of insecurity and doubt.

In a marriage, you can also leave lasting pictures of love for your husband or wife. Your gentle acts of touch, no matter how small, can impart an indelible image of commitment and unconditional acceptance that supports an intimate marriage for a lifetime.

Security, meaningful communication, romantic/ emotional experiences, and meaningful acts of touch —all four are pillars upon which a fulfilling marriage is built. And all four, when strengthened by word pictures, can help span the differences and disagreements that can wash away a couple's marriage vows.

There is one final pillar upon which all the others depend—the pillar of spiritual intimacy. Without it, a couple can miss God's power to transform hearts and lives. Listen to the beautiful word picture, intended as a musical chorus, found in the Bible, the most inspiring source of word pictures:

> Blessed are all who fear the Lord,
>   who walk in his ways . . .
> Your wife will be like a fruitful vine
>   within your house;
> your sons will be like olive shoots
>   around your table.[13]

What an incredible description of the rewards that await husbands and wives who are energized by faith in God! We're so convinced of the importance of this marital support that we've written an entire book about it. *Joy That Lasts*[14] describes how to find fulfillment—more than our cup can hold. Such a life can free us from our selfishness to build the bridge of intimacy that will last forever.

Those who enjoy an intimate, secure, romantic marriage have learned about bridge building. And as we've mentioned, word pictures are a key tool in the process. They're also crucial with our children. From experience with our own children and with families across the world, we've learned that word pictures aren't an elective—they're a requirement. To show what we mean, let's turn our attention to how word pictures can aid moms and dads. Without a doubt, parents who master the language of love possess a key that can open their child's heart.

We've watched with amazement the many times our children have responded to emotional word pictures of praise, discipline, and love. That's why we discuss in the next chapter how to use them to balance two crucial parenting skills.

CHAPTER THIRTEEN

Gaining Higher Ground as a Parent

In the past fifteen years, we've seen two aspects of parenting consistently generate the most frustration and disharmony in a home. They top the list when it comes to counseling letters we receive, and keep us busy nonstop during coffee breaks at conferences.

What are these two parenting concerns? The first is a ten-letter word that has become a dirty word in many homes—discipline. Discipline problems can cause an unhealthy pendulum swing between a permissive and restrictive parent. It can leave the mother feeling like a policewoman in the home, the father like a broken record.

Isn't there a better way to raise a child than raising our voices? Isn't there an alternative to giving Lecture #202 which the kids have memorized? They even correct you if you skip part of it!

We wholeheartedly recommend several books on the subject of discipline.¹ Yet, when it comes to this crucial area of parenting, there's one tool that is often overlooked. This tool, a word picture, grabs children's emotions and delivers a message of lasting conviction to their hearts.

Does that sound too easy? The next time you're tempted to apply the "board of education" to your child's seat of learning, try a word picture first. It can pack a tremendous emotional wallop.

That's exactly what I (Gary) discovered years ago with my oldest son, Greg. Though I didn't realize it at the time, the story I shared with him instantly stopped an unwanted behavior and still helps to shape a positive relationship between us.

Getting Back on the Team

When Greg was twelve, a problem surfaced between us that I couldn't ignore. It dealt with his reaction whenever I flew out of town for a speaking engagement.

On the day I was to leave, everyone in the family would help me pack. Then, at the door, they would always send me off with a "Go get 'em, Dad!" or "We'll miss you!"

However, when Greg entered the sixth grade, I noticed that he no longer was a vital part of the going-away party. Instead of lingering at the door with the rest of the family, he would walk away. Soon, his behavior wasn't limited to avoiding me on my outbound trip. For several hours after I returned, he would often keep his distance.

As time passed, he went to great, creative lengths to give me the cold shoulder. Even when I tried to catch him for a moment of conversation, his words were frigid. "Later, Dad," he would cut me off. "I've got to go over to one of my friend's now."

As a counselor, I realized his actions largely reflected his feelings about my traveling. But I also realized I couldn't abandon my monthly trips and still feed my family. Plus, allowing him to ignore me at home and letting his anger build up when I left wasn't doing either one of us any good.

Furthermore, I didn't want him to develop a pattern of ignoring others when he was upset with them. Nor did I want him perfecting a negative habit that could easily carry over into his friendships and, later, his marriage. Most of all, I missed his friendship and didn't want this problem to become a permanent wedge in our relationship.

So I decided I would practice what I teach. On the next flight home, I came up with a word picture for him. I knew it would be effective, because I had seen others work over the years in hundreds of adults' lives. But I had never tried to use them as a corrective tool with my children.

After the conversation I had with my son, word pictures became a permanent part of our parenting plan. In the years to come, I would use them with each of my children—and still do. With word pictures, I saw more positive change in less time than from any lecture I had ever given.

If you're a parent who wants some extra ammunition for dealing with a problem situation, word pictures can help. I know, because the imaginary story of an all-star basketball player kept my son's attention, right to the final buzzer.

It had been two days since I had returned home from my latest business trip. Sure enough, Greg was playing emotional hide-and-seek, but didn't want me to find him.

As was my custom, I would often wake up one of the children early Saturday morning, and then we would go out together for breakfast. This morning, it was Greg's turn.

When I first woke him, I could tell by the look in his

eyes and the way he shrank back from my touch that he was still upset. But when I mentioned going to his favorite breakfast spot, I put a choke hold on any ideas he might have had to avoid me.

Later, as we sat at the table enjoying stacks of pancakes and syrup, I began sharing my word picture.

"Greg," I said, looking him in the eye, "I need to explain something to you, and I'd like to start by telling you a short story. Are you up for it?"

"Sure, Dad, fire away," he replied, swallowing a mouthful of pancakes.

"Let's say you were a star basketball player on the junior high squad."

It was the time of year for the college basketball championship. Like me, Greg was a rabid fan and remained glued to the television from the opening tip-off of the Final Four. With popcorn bowl in hand, he watched nearly every game of the NCAA tournament.

For years, I'd shot baskets with him and watched him practice, practice, practice by himself on our backboard at home. I knew the goal of his backyard heroics was to be good enough one day to be the star of the varsity team.

With all this in mind, I had selected and practiced a word picture that I thought would grab his interest. I certainly hit the bull's-eye as I continued.

"For half the season, you've been the high-point man on your team and the leader in assists as well. Your fellow players and the fans love you so much that every time you go out on the court, they yell, 'Greg-O!' 'Greg-O!' 'Greg-O!' "

My chanting his name in the restaurant brought a quick smile to his face as he devoured another pancake.

"Then one game, you twist your neck pulling down a rebound, and it's really sore the next day. In fact, it gets so stiff that Mom takes you out of school and into the doctor's office.

"After looking you over, the doc says you must wear a plastic neck brace and can't play or practice for the next three weeks. Sitting out of the games is the hardest thing you've ever done. You can only watch your teammates from the stands and dream about playing alongside them.

"Twenty-one long days and nights later, you're finally ready to throw away the neck brace and get back on the team again. But something happens your first day back at practice.

"Instead of the players crowding around, cheering and telling you how glad they are you're back, they ignore you! The guy who took your place is especially cool. Even the coach acts like you never were that important to the team and doesn't put you into games like he did before your injury."

From the moment I mentioned basketball, I could see in his eyes that I had picked the one subject that captured his interest more than what he was eating. I had done the impossible. He had actually put down his fork to listen to my story.

"If something like that happened to you, Big Guy, how would it make you feel?"

"I'd feel terrible, Dad. I'd want to get back on the team."

Returning his look, I paused before saying, "Greg, do you realize that at least once a month you're treating me like this coach treated you in my story?"

"No! I'm not doing anything like that," he said emphatically. "I love you, Dad. I'd never try to make you feel terrible."

"Greg, I know you don't realize it, but every time I leave on a trip, you act just like those guys on the team. For several hours after I'm back home, you reject me and don't want to let me back on the family team.

"If my boss tells me I have to go out of town and miss three days at home, you often keep me out of the game when I get back. Like the guy in the story, it hurts to be sitting on the bench—especially when I don't understand why you won't let me back in the game.

"Greg, I want to be a part of your life. I want to get back on your team when I come home. It hurts being rejected by you, and it's not doing you any good to build up anger against me."

That morning at the table, I saw the light of conviction and understanding dawn on my son's face. He was so caught up in the emotions my story generated that he said he was sorry for ignoring me. Even more spectacular, he assured me things would be different from that moment on. He still wasn't crazy about me traveling, but he said he would never again purposely ignore me.

To be honest, as we drove home and I listened to my son's promises about the future, I couldn't help thinking, *This all sounds great, but he's only twelve! There's no way he's going to remember this.*

However, the first test of my doubts came all too soon. Only a few weeks had passed when I was packing my bags. But this time, along with the rest of the family, Greg helped me get ready. And like everyone else, he even hugged me before I left.

I walked outside feeling surprised, relieved, and thankful for my son's change of attitude. Just as I reached the car and started to open the door, he called to me from the front porch. With that classic grin of his, he said, "Have a great trip, Dad. And get ready to be rejected when you get home!"

When I got back from my trip, he didn't ignore me.

And he never has since. As the result of one shared breakfast and a word picture used to sweeten the conversation, we dealt with a problem that could have mushroomed into an angry, distant relationship between father and son. Once again, I saw the personal value of using word pictures with children.

An emotional word picture can help sharpen and extend your parenting skills by maximizing your words. It also helps you whittle many problems down to size.

An emotional word picture can help sharpen and extend your parenting skills by maximizing your words. It also helps you whittle many problems down to size.

A Second Parenting Frustration: Losing Perspective in Tough Times

Dr. James Dobson, a noted psychologist, has written an excellent book, *Parenting Isn't for Cowards.*[2] We love the title and the book, primarily because it talks openly about the courage it takes to be an effective parent—especially during tough times. In particular, the book discusses the kind of courage it takes during the uphill years with two-year-olds and teenagers, and the struggle parents face with letting go as their children grow up.

If there's a subject we get asked about as frequently as discipline, it's facing those two difficult stages. That being the case, how can a word picture help parents gain the patience and encouragement to face a problem age or to "hang in there" during a difficult time?

Let's listen to the word picture one young woman

used to give us an answer. For years, this woman dreamed of being a mother. Yet the very day her dream came true, it was also shattered. It wasn't until she put her feelings into a word picture that she finally got a handle on her emotions and expectations.

Her word picture has given her the hope and courage to continue being the best parent she can be, even when she's tempted to collapse inside. Here's the moving word picture she expressed to us:

"I had always dreamed of owning a beautiful vase —an expensive one, hand-crafted just for me with exquisite curves and intricate details," she began.

"I spent hours thinking of where it would best fit in my house and how proudly I'd display it. I'd picture it being the first thing a relative or guest would see. It would capture their eyes and generate their praise.

"Finally, the day came when I was to pick up my precious vase. Neither the years of waiting nor the pain of its price tag could dampen my joy—until I was handed a crushed vase.

"Instead of the work of art I'd seen in my mind for so long, I was given a vase that was shattered into a thousand pieces. My heart was broken into as many pieces, and I cried long after my tears had run dry.

"For days, I felt there must have been a mistake. Surely someone else deserved a broken vase, not me. But slowly, painfully, I pulled myself together. That process began the day I held the broken pieces in my hands and vowed to put them back together. Although I realized the vase would never be perfect, I knew that I could love it, cracks and all.

"Little by little, the pile of pieces started to take shape. As the days went by, I gathered more love and patience to glue them together than I ever thought possible. In time, I began to see a masterpiece growing from what had been a mess.

"But that doesn't mean things have been easy. Two groups of people keep coming back time and again.

"The first group is larger and louder than I ever imagined. Every time these people walk by, they go out of their way to step on some of the broken pieces. They crush and grind them into the ground with their cruel words and contemptuous stares—until the pieces seem beyond repair. I always feel so helpless and frustrated when they parade by. I wish they'd leave and never come back, but they always return. With them around, I'm again tempted to see only broken pieces and smeared glue, not a priceless vase.

"The second group is much smaller, but has a heart twice as large. Seeing the shattered pieces, these people kneel beside me and gently help me pick them up. One by one, they carefully help me fit each piece into place—almost as if it were their vase. Unlike the first group, these people leave me filled with renewed hope and love.

"If you haven't realized it yet, the vase I'm talking about is my precious, handicapped child.

"I had always wanted a baby. But I was devastated when the doctor said she'd never be 'normal.' My husband and I asked God to give us a special love for our daughter, and He has. Of course, there are days when I tire of picking up the pieces. But somehow the work is easier now. So much love and commitment have already gone into cementing her life together that I can't imagine loving anyone or anything more."

For this young woman, picturing her precious child as a priceless vase helped her think through her feelings of love, hope, anger, confusion, and grief. It also gave us a graphic picture of what was going on in her life.

When the parenting task gets tough, emotional word pictures can flesh out hidden feelings and give parents an entirely new perspective. It can help lift their eyes above their circumstances and give them a vise-like grip on their feelings.

The first two hurdles that trip parents are those of discipline and maintaining a positive attitude during tough times. Like an expert coach, word pictures can help you get over these barriers in winning form. In addition, word pictures can assist parents four other ways.

Not only can they help you get over the hurdles, but they can help you raise blue-ribbon children as well. They provide a legacy of love your children can carry with them for a lifetime.

CHAPTER FOURTEEN

Building Blocks to Successful Parenting

Over several years, we researched and wrote a book on how parents can most effectively communicate love and high value to their children. In writing the book, entitled *The Blessing,* we learned a great deal about the skills of unconditionally loving and encouraging children.[1] Unfortunately, we also unearthed far more than we ever wanted to know about children who grew up with critical disapproval.

When we wrote the book, we knew the failure to communicate love and acceptance was an issue in many homes. Yet, we had no idea of its magnitude. Since *The Blessing* was released, we've heard from hundreds of people who, as children, never felt loved or valued by their parents. As a result, they often left home and walked right into alcoholism, substance abuse, chronic depression, workaholism, and shattered marriage and parent/child relationships of their own.[2] These problems are all echoes of their unhappiness from childhood.

In an attempt to run away from a family in which

they didn't feel loved, many adolescents have also dashed right into the arms of cult members and damaging sexual relationships. They have left far behind the moral, spiritual, and religious values of their parents.[3]

We know that as a concerned parent, you would never want to see any of these problems crop up in your child's life. But then, neither did the parents of those we've received letters from—each of whom is now living in emotional pain.

Many parents thought they were making deposit after deposit into their child's love bank, only to have that child leave home feeling like he or she had a zero balance deep inside. In fact, the majority of letters we receive are not from physically abused children or from alcoholic homes. Often the most tragic stories are from boys and girls who grew up in families that were loving in many ways—yet their love wasn't communicated in a manner that was understood and accepted.

How could this happen? What makes the difference between a home that sends a child out into life feeling valued, loved, and blessed, and a home that doesn't? Often it lies in what was said by the parents—or not said.

Children desperately need to know—and to hear in ways they understand and remember—that they're loved and valued by Mom and Dad. How can you communicate the high value and acceptance you have for your children in a special way? How can you share words that protect and provide for them? How can you better understand them, and have them understand you?

Again, we know of no better way for you to leave a legacy of love for your children than to use emotional word pictures.

Word pictures can help a parent say "I love you"
in a manner a child can't miss.

Providing a Legacy of Love for Your Children

As we mentioned in the previous chapters, the reason many people don't build intimate marriages is because they lack the necessary knowledge and skills. The same thing is true with effective parenting. It, too, takes knowledge and skills—knowing what breaks relationships down and being able to build them up.

You've already seen how word pictures can help in the important parenting areas of discipline and positive attitude. In the pages that follow, we want to share with you four additional ways in which word pictures can help a parent say "I love you" in a manner a child can't miss. They're reflections of the pillars that hold up an intimate marriage, which we discussed in chapters eleven and twelve.

But before we launch into the various ways word pictures help parents, we must face another problem. For in many homes, it isn't a lack of skills that's the issue. It's the lack of time.

"I've Got All the Time in the World . . ."

If a common cry for many children is, "Please say you love me," an equally common response by many parents is, "I've got all the time in the world to tell you." Really? We wish that were true!

What would you do if you walked into a doctor's office one day and were told you had Lou Gehrig's disease? How would you react to the black-and-white words that you would be dead in twenty months or less?

If you had spent almost all your waking hours learning skills to build a career, how could you begin to switch your focus to building an intimate relationship with your wife and children? If you knew that, in a short time, all your family would have was a memory of you, how could you leave a legacy of love for them to embrace? Most of all, how could you leave your wife and children words that would warm their hearts, even when you were no longer able to pull them close and wrap them in your arms?

If you were a friend of ours, whom we'll call Steve, you would really have to answer these questions. They're all things he's heard and thought. They're all real-life questions he's facing now, even as we write this book.

Steve has three children and a loving wife. And he's dying of amyotrophic lateral sclerosis, a rare and fatal disease best known for bringing down Lou Gehrig, the "iron man" of baseball.[4]

I (John) met Steve at a family camp where I was speaking. Unlike those who had come for vacation, he came with another purpose in mind. He didn't have long to live and wanted his life—and his words—to count.

As I spoke about practical ways to build value into relationships, Steve took detailed notes. After the presentation, we sat down and talked about an idea he had—an idea to capture his love and prayers for his family through word pictures.

He won't always be able to look into his children's eyes. Yet, over the years, their eyes can read and reread a series of letters he's working on right now—a collection of word pictures that will be waiting for them to open at important times in their lives.

He won't have the chance to be one of the proud

parents seated at his children's high school graduation, but his words will be there.

He'll miss the excitement of packing up his son's and daughters' car as they head off for their first day of college, but his message of encouragement will be there.

He'll never have the opportunity to walk his daughters down the aisle on their weddings or receive the phone call that he's just become a grandfather, but his pictures of love and support will be there.

That's because he's writing word pictures now that will carry his prayers, wishes and hopes for them in the future—where his voice won't reach.

By the time this book finds its way into your hands, Steve may already be in the hands of God. Yet his family will always have his personal legacy of love—word pictures that are so vivid and real they will seem to become flesh, complete with arms to hug and hold his wife and children. Through these words, his presence will bless and encourage his family for a lifetime.

Moms and dads, what's your reason for not speaking the words your children need to hear so much? Are your other activities really so important that you can't speak or write down words your children can treasure for a lifetime? We may not have a medical clock ticking behind us. But for each of us, it's later than we think.

With the light speed at which children grow up and with the very real uncertainties of life, this is no time to withhold words of love and affection. There's too much at stake in their future for you to put off learning the skills that can make a lasting difference in their lives.

For whatever reason, let's all stop procrastinating and start looking at four ways emotional word pictures can carry our message of love straight to their hearts, beginning with the pillar of security.

Word Pictures and Parenting

1. Children Need Security in Words and Actions.

A few years ago, we counseled with a husband and wife who were constantly fighting. Try as we might, we couldn't seem to help bring an end to their heated arguments.

Whenever we think we're getting nowhere with a couple, there's something we do that always puts things in a new perspective. That is, we ask the couple to bring their children to the next session.

Over the years, we've discovered that children are God's little spies! Mom and Dad may be able to snow us and walk around issues. But when we invite the kids, in an unguarded moment they'll walk you right up to what you most need to know.

When we sat down with this couple at our next session, we were joined by their handsome eleven-year-old son and darling six-year-old daughter. And while we didn't realize it at the time, we were about to be given a tremendous lesson about the importance of security in a home.

"What bothers you the most about your parents' arguing?" we asked their daughter.

She looked quickly over to her parents. When her mother nodded, the little girl said, "Every time Daddy gets mad at Mommy or us, he takes off his wedding ring and throws it away."

Her father quickly explained that he wasn't literally throwing away his wedding ring. He was just "venting" his anger. When something set him off, he would pull off his ring and make it ricochet off a few walls. He then explained away what he was doing as a "healthy expression" of anger. After all, he said, we were counselors and would know how damaging it was to hold anger inside.

What he didn't realize was that his actions had become a word picture of instant insecurity to his daughter. By ripping off his ring, he conveyed a symbol to her that was projected in technicolor on a forty-foot screen in her mind. His action represented all the fear this little girl had that he would hurt or desert the family.

Every time this precious little one saw her daddy's wedding ring get thrown across the room, she saw her future sail away with it. Instead of building the security that she so desperately needed, her father created for her a world of constant fear. This fear, brought on by lack of security, ate at her stomach so badly that she had already been diagnosed as having childhood ulcers.[5]

For more than a year before they had come in for counseling, her father's wedding ring was a word picture for desertion, loneliness, fear, and anxiety. That began to change only when he was confronted with the damage he was doing.

We began "milking" the young girl's word picture (a skill we discussed earlier in the book)[6] by asking her father questions, such as:

"What causes you so much frustration around the house that you pull off your ring and throw it?"

"When you were growing up, did you see your father—literally or figuratively—pull off his wedding ring?"

"How close do you think your wife is to pulling off her ring?"

"How do you think it makes the kids feel when they see your ring go flying?" and

"What would it take, beginning right now, to put the ring back on your finger and always keep it there?"

Through the word picture of a ring, we spoke to an entire family about the subject of security. Because we tied into a word picture in their home, our words grabbed the father's emotions like nothing we'd said in all the previous sessions.

While not every story has a happy ending, this one did. At the conclusion of their time in counseling a few months later, this family did two things.

First, they took the time to share a word picture with their children about a wedding ring that had been scarred and dented, but now had been repaired and brightly polished. And they assured their children that the ring would stay on both Mom's and Dad's fingers, no matter what they faced in the future.

This wise couple knew they had not built a foundation of security for their children, and willingly admitted they had caused their children physical and emotional damage. That's what brought them into counseling. There they opened up to needed changes when their daughter pointed out a word picture to them.

Their little girl now has a very different picture in her mind of Daddy's ring. No longer does it stand for anger, frustration, and fear. Instead, it shines with the love, courage, and resolve needed to work through problems. His words, together with his actions, repainted the faded picture of an unstable home into a masterpiece of security.

On a one-to-ten scale, how's the security level around your home these days? If it's slipped into the threes and fours, you're communicating a word picture of insecurity to your children.

When it comes to parenting, kids don't bloom and grow if their roots are constantly ripped out. Insecurity in a home pulls out roots; security provides the depth and shelter for them to thrive.

If you're a single parent, you have ten times the

reason to assure your child that you won't leave him or her, and word pictures can help. In any separation or divorce, children get a massive dose of insecurity. To combat the negative damage of such feelings, you must provide a constant source of security. In a later chapter, we'll share a treasury of more than 100 word pictures to help you do that very thing.

We've seen how important security is, both for our children and marriage. Now let's look at how we can use word pictures to build character in our sons and daughters.

2. Children Need Instruction and Friendship.

It's clear that with young children, the greatest way to bring change is through instruction that builds character. Educators have known this for years. That's one reason that figurative language and word pictures are a key to teaching younger children.

From preschool on, children learn and remember lessons better if they are communicated with a story or object.[7] In fact, one early sign of a learning disability for a grade school child is his or her inability to understand figures of speech.[8] It isn't only modern-day research that supports this use of word pictures to instruct children.

Since ancient times, a parent's goal revolved around "training up a child in the way he should go."[9] As the primary shapers of a child's character, parents do well to spend time instructing young children in ways that would provide a healthy platform for later life.[10]

How do children best understand abstract concepts, such as honesty, truthfulness, discipline, and love? Whether it's an educational concept or a spiritual truth, children (or adults) learn best when a word picture is part of the instruction time.

Parents with young children can find a ready-made application of the research studies and history we've already mentioned in this book. That is, word pictures are a key to building character and helping us communicate our point. In large part, that's because emotional stories take on the qualities of real life, especially with children.

This is one reason television viewing should be so closely monitored. It's also one reason a word picture, drawn from one of the four wells, can be so powerful.

We know of one mother who used her microwave oven to teach her son a much needed lesson about anger. She took a clear plastic mug, filled it with water, and set the microwave on high for three minutes. As she and her son watched the calm surface of the water be transformed into raging bubbles, she talked with him about handling his frustration.

She asked her young son what made him boil over inside at times. Then they talked about how he could push the "pause" button and talk to her when things began frustrating him. That way she could help him with his frustration in its early stages, instead of hearing about it when he was boiling over with emotions.

Another mother drew upon a biblical proverb—a type of word picture—to talk with her very unmotivated child. The proverb says, "Go to the ant, you sluggard: consider its ways."[11]

After a good deal of thought, this wise woman made her son do just that. She bought him an ant farm and got him excited about capturing, feeding, and watching the nonstop activity of a colony. Every day, her son observed how the ants all worked together and stayed at a task. In so doing, he saw living examples of character traits his mother wanted to build into his life.

In an appropriate time and way, she used a word picture with him. She talked about how he could be a better "ant" with his household chores and school-work, and how what he did or didn't do around the house affected everyone else. To her immense surprise, he began making tangible changes in his behavior.

In these homes and hundreds of others, the parents have used word pictures to bring lessons to life for their youngsters. They know that when a child has a picture of a desired behavior—instead of just words—he learns a lesson faster and remembers it longer than the most inspired lecture they can give.[12]

Mastering word pictures with young children is crucial. That's because their little minds are still in the "input" stage where they're most open to change through instruction. But soon, with the onset of puberty, a youngster will move to the "I've-already-got-the-answers" stage. Adolescence requires a different approach to accomplish change.

Using Word Pictures with Adolescents

Teenagers usually go through an "individuality crisis" just about the time their parents go through the midlife "identity crisis." What's the result of this emotional mismatch? As a man once said, "What we have here is a failure to communicate!"

If the goal of parents with young children is character building through instruction, their goal with adolescents is building through friendship.

Discipline takes on a new meaning when you're looking up at your son, instead of down at him. And when your daughter's friends all drive cars, it's hard to keep her around the house long enough to hear your hour-long speeches. By a child's teen years, parents often reap the results of the character instruction—both good and bad—they sowed earlier. But if that's the case, how do you change a teenager's behavior? Again, word pictures hold a powerful key.

Researchers point out that for adults (teens are adults in their thinking process, if not always in their judgment), the best way to change someone is through a significant emotional event.[13] Think about this for a moment.

When are adults most teachable? When a significant event impacts an important relationship.

We've seen a husband who wouldn't crack a marriage enrichment book devour dozens of them when his wife walked out.

We've seen a woman who never wrote a letter home suddenly write nonstop notes after receiving the news her mother was dying.

And we've seen teenagers listen to words of praise, instruction, and correction with the greatest effect, when expressed by a parent who is also their friend. It's a wise father or mother who doesn't rely only on grounding or grabbing away car keys, but who can grab a child's emotions in a heart-to-heart conversation.

If you're like many parents and have declared war on your teenager, we can assure you there will be no winners—only prisoners. And if a teenager is a captive in his own home, watch out when he breaks the chains and goes off to college or work.

If you're more interested in your son's behavior than his character, he'll pick up the inconsistency. If your daughter senses you're more concerned that she doesn't embarrass you than that she does what's best for her, you'll get resistance. And if you don't know what it takes to develop a meaningful friendship with your child, then your first priority should be to get the necessary knowledge and skills.[14]

You can force a two-year-old to sit down on the outside . . . even if he or she is standing up on the inside! But you can't force-feed words and ideas down teenagers' throats and expect them not to react and regurgitate those words later.

In a home where a parent and child can't be friends, teens will listen to their peer group instead of you. If you want to be the one who has your son's or daughter's ear, then try learning their language. Try speaking the language of love. The music they listen to does. Their peers do. Even the Bible they read does. If you want to make inroads of friendship with your child, then you will, too.

Whether we have young children in the instructional stage or the friendship-building years, word pictures help us as parents. A brief look at the remaining two reflections from the pillars of marriage can help as well.

3. Children Need the Love That Meaningful Touch Can Bring.

In the chapter on building an intimate marriage, we noted that meaningful touch can greatly impact any relationship. In a very real sense, it leaves a word picture of commitment and caring in another person's mind. But is this also true with children?

We recently heard from a young, single-parent mother who had read one of our parenting books. In one of the chapters, we stress the symbolic picture that touch gives a child, and it convicted her right down to her socks.

This young woman, whom we'll call Julie, had become pregnant out of wedlock. Believing life was sacred, she opted to carry her baby to term and not kill him. She had initially decided on adoption, but at the last minute she decided to keep her newborn son, Jason.

After the excitement of having a newborn wore off, problems began to develop. As the baby grew older, so did her resentment of him. Instead of a joy, he became a burden. Instead of an object to love, he became a symbol of her frustration with life.

But she began to head down a different path when she started going to a church near her small apartment. Members took her under their wing and helped her in every way. Yet she still felt deep resentment toward Jason that she couldn't seem to shake. That emotion manifested itself in one particular way—she didn't want to touch him.

Touch is the first way babies know they are loved. Long before they can understand words, they clearly read the nonverbal language of love, expressed through meaningful touch. But that was missing from the pages of Jason's little life.

What changed Julie? What made her open to going against her feelings and reaching out for her son?

As he grew older, she began noticing problems in his life that she couldn't ignore. After reading in our book about the incredible power of meaningful touch, she talked with a group of close friends about the repulsion she felt toward her son. Wisely, they encouraged her to talk further with a counselor.

Within a few sessions, Julie was confronted with many reasons why she withheld meaningful touch: guilt from the past; a lack of touch in her own home; the fact that Jason looked very much like his father— the man who had gotten her pregnant and then laughed at her plans to keep the baby.

Finally, she decided to give her son a picture of the love she had for him—through physical touch. But her first attempts didn't go quite as she'd expected. When she reached out to hug him, he ran away! She'd only touched him before when she was angry. So when she put her arms around him he fled, crying in confusion and fear.

However, after several weeks, Julie's determination to offer this powerful picture of love won out. And the transformation in Jason's attitude and actions was dramatic. Not only did her son become more sociable and less anxious around others, but his schoolwork and attention span in class also improved! All because she began giving him a powerful, nonverbal word picture of her love for him.

On a scale of one to ten, how high would your children rate you for touching them in meaningful ways? Have you asked them lately? Have you ever asked your spouse that question?

Even with teenagers who cringe when their mom or dad hugs them ("Oh, Mom, stop that! One of my friends might see you!"), they still need that picture of love. You may have to get a little creative (try wrestling on the carpet!). But you build love and value in a child when you're not afraid or don't neglect to touch your children in meaningful ways.

4. Children Need Times of Emotional Bonding.

We realize that "romantic/emotionally bonding" times that are so important in a marriage have definite limits with a child. However, if you drop the word "romantic," you should have all the emotional bonding you can with your son or daughter!

The best way we know to bond within a family is by going camping. It's not the act of camping that provides closeness, but what happens when we camp with our kids. You guessed it: catastrophes!

For some reason, the memories of a camping trip— where you forgot all the food but the marshmallows; where the tent collapsed for no reason—twice; where you had a blow-out on the way up and a blow-up on the way back home—all can become great bonding experiences.

You'll never forget the time you went out for ice cream and had your little one's cone drop on his shoe! And how can you forget the time you took the older one surfing for the first time and then paid for the stitches when the board sliced open his chin? Such experiences not only bond us (after the stitches have healed, of course), but travel right to a child's heart.

By this point in the book you've seen the "whys" and "how-tos" of using word pictures in your important relationships. Soon we'll close the book by giving you 101 word pictures that you can begin to apply immediately. Yet before we reach this treasury of word pictures, there's something we can't overlook.

Misusing word pictures is a danger we'd rather ignore, but can't. Over the years we've seen dramatic examples of the good that's come from using the language of love. But we've also seen great emotional destruction come when it's misused or twisted into a language of hate.

We don't relish the look. But we feel it's important to pull back the shades and expose those who would exploit the dark side of emotional word pictures. These are people who emotionally (or physically) hurt others time and again. They repel any word pictures you give them, and turn theirs on you like an attacking pit bull terrier. They are the kind of people who can't seem to love back.

HOW CAN
WORD PICTURES
HELP MY WALK WITH GOD?

CHAPTER FIFTEEN

Using Emotional Word Pictures to Strengthen Your Spiritual Life

Since this book was first published, one of our greatest joys has been to receive letters that tell how a word picture has benefited someone. An especially encouraging report arrived a while back that described one of the most unusual uses of a word picture we've ever heard.

Broken Bottles . . . Shattered Lives

Imagine you're ministering to those at the very bottom of society's ladder. Seated in front of you are several rows of dirty, downcast, skid-row alcoholics. While a few might be at your rescue mission out of a pure desire to hear about God's free gift of grace, most are there because they know that once you finish your sermon, they'll get a free, hot meal.

Like many on the homeless trail, these men have heard the gospel message countless times, from countless preachers, in countless shelters across the country. And while familiarity with the gospel might put words of faith in their mouths, their minds are on physical, not spiritual, nourishment.

Interested in getting up and trying to motivate *this* crowd?

That was the situation facing Chaplain Bill one cold November night. He knew the challenge before him, and it frustrated him. How could he break through to those men's hardened hearts with the light of God's love? How could he tell the old, old story in a way that brought a new response of faith?

Chaplain Bill always worked hard on his talks. But in preparing to speak to his castaway congregation this week, he had come across a new communication tool he couldn't wait to try.

Bill had just finished reading the first edition of the book you hold in your hands. With a strong inner conviction, he believed a word picture was just what he needed to break through the barriers that the hard edge of life has put on his "parishioners'" lives. So he prepared to do something he'd never done before in a sermon.

Standing before the men, Bill pulled something out from behind the podium as he began to speak.

An Unlikely Picture of Unconditional Love

"Okay, men, what's this I'm holding?" Bill asked with a mischievous grin.

Slowly, he drew something out of a brown paper sack. As the hidden item came into view, a chorus of laughter swept across the room.

"You've got yourself a bottle, Rev!" one man shouted.

"I've seen a few of those!" another said with a laugh as the familiar green glass of a cheap wine bottle was brought into sight.

"That's right, men," Bill said, looking out on his smiling audience. "I've got a bottle here. Now, let me tell you a little about myself, and then I want to tell you a story about this bottle—and what happened to it."

The crowd was unusually attentive as Bill continued. "Instead of finishing high school, I joined the Navy at seventeen. After ten years in the service, I made petty officer and was doing real well. I had a fine wife, a good job, and a family. I even had a house I was paying on. But then my wife was killed in an accident, and I was left alone with the two young kids.

"It was like my heart died when she did, and I took to drinking hard. In less than two years, I had turned myself into such a problem the Navy discharged me. Then I lost my kids to the state because I was neglecting them due to the drinking, and things just got worse from there.

"You see, my life was a lot like this little bottle here. I always thought I was going to be something special. Maybe I'd be used to hold some special medicine, or I might be made into a fine piece of china to set in some rich person's house. But when it came right down to it, I ended up just a plain, green bottle, sent down a conveyor belt and filled with cheap wine.

"I was packed with a bunch of other bottles and shipped to a big city. There I sat on a dark, dusty shelf for a long time. And while that was bad, something worse finally happened; an old wino pulled me off the shelf and carried me out back into a dark alley.

"Three of his drinking buddies met him there, and they all passed me around and finished me off. Finally, that old wino staggered to his feet. Swaying side to side, he drew back and heaved me into a brick wall, smashing me to pieces.

"That's where my life was, men," Chaplain Bill said. "And for a long time, I lay there in that alley, so shattered and mixed in with all the other broken bottles that I knew there was no way the pieces of my life could ever come back together."

Shifting his weight and looking the men in the eyes, he continued, "But I was wrong."

Chaplain Bill told us that by this point in his weekly sermon, he's usually preaching to nodding heads and frozen smiles or hearing snide remarks about getting on to dinner. But not that night. "No one was saying anything," he said, "and the eyes of every man in that room were riveted on me." He went on with his story.

"For what seemed like a lifetime, I lay in that alley, all out of hope. Then suddenly, I saw a dark shape coming toward me. Whoever it was actually kneeled down in that dirty, smelly alley and began sifting through all those broken pieces.

"How He did it, I don't know, but that Man found all my shattered pieces, one by one. And starting with my heart, He pieced me back together. It's been five years since He found me in that alley, and He's been polishing away at the cracks ever since."

Choked with emotion as the memories flooded back, Bill finished his talk with an invitation.

"I know what you men are like on the inside," he said. "I was just as broken up as you are—just as hopeless, just as filled with doubt that anything or anyone could ever piece my life back together.

"But there's someone who can make you whole— the same Man who sought me out and found me in that dark alley." Holding up the bottle, Bill continued, "His name is Jesus, and you can know Him as your personal Lord and Savior. You can have Him put the pieces of your life back together, like He did for me—and He can do it tonight."

Bill's sermon was over, and the response he got staggered him. With smells of dinner wafting up from the kitchen below, no one stirred from his seat. The usually rambunctious crowd was quiet as the men thought through what the chaplain had said. And while such services often yield no visible results, that night there was rejoicing in heaven—two men came to know the One who made them and who alone could put their lives back together. Several others rededicated their lives to the Restorer of their souls.

Why did a word picture work so well in communicating spiritual truth to those men? Actually, it shouldn't surprise us that word pictures are so powerful a tool. The pages of Scripture are filled with them, and emotional word pictures can help strengthen our spiritual lives in four major ways.

1. Word Pictures Can Draw Us Closer to God

Imagine living in a small, rural town, and in all your life, you've never driven more than a few miles from home. If you were asked to put yourself in the shoes of the president of the United States, with all his traveling and international networking, understanding who he is and what he does could seem impossible. But read a newspaper, turn on the television, or subscribe to a news magazine, and suddenly the whole world of public events is at your doorstep. You can even see pictures of the president's travels, and you feel closer to him as a result.

Words and pictures can help us bridge the distance between a politician and an everyday citizen. Yet for all time, finite people have struggled even more in trying to bridge the immense gap between themselves and a God who is all-powerful and all-knowing.

The psalmist wrote of God, "The Lord has established his throne in heaven,"[1] and through the prophet God Himself proclaimed, "My thoughts are not your thoughts, neither are your ways my ways."[2]

How dare we draw near to such a powerful God?

Thankfully, He took the initiative in revealing Himself to us. We see the invisible God most clearly in the visible expression of His Son. And throughout the Scriptures, emotional word pictures provide the best means of getting to know Him and communicating His love to others.

Consider parents who want to bring God's love up close to a child. Where will many of them turn? To Psalm 23, where they can read to their little lambs, "The Lord is my shepherd, I shall not be in want. He makes me lie down in green pastures."³

Those same fathers and mothers, when faced with the inevitable tragedies of life, will often turn to the same passage to catch a glimpse of their loving Shepherd: "Even though I walk through the valley of the shadow of death, I will fear no evil, for you are with me; your rod and your staff, they comfort me."⁴

Word pictures have always made God more accessible, more real, and more understandable to our finite minds. Perhaps that's one reason Jesus employed them so much.

Our Lord's primary teaching style was to use *parables*. Word pictures filled His messages to the crowds and disciples alike. On any given day, you could hear stories about the good Samaritan, the fig tree, the lost coin, and the lost sheep. At other times, He would issue great challenges by talking about different types of soil, buried or invested talents, and the need for His followers to pick up their own crosses and follow Him.

Jesus also described Himself as the Good Shepherd, the Door, the Way, and the Truth. He was called the Cornerstone, Bread, and Living Water, to cite just a few examples.

The Picture Behind the Verse

While many of Jesus' word pictures are well known, others go overlooked. And perhaps the most neglected word picture Christ used in describing Himself comes just before one of the most familiar verses in all the Bible.

The first verse many people memorize after becoming Christians is John 3:16: "For God so loved the world that he gave his one and only Son, that whoever believes in him shall not perish but have eternal life."

But do you know what John 3:*14-15* says?

Jesus had been speaking to Nicodemus at night, answering the fearful Pharisee's questions regarding salvation. He heard from Jesus that he would need to be born again. When Nicodemus couldn't comprehend the necessity to be born physically *and* spiritually, Jesus called to his mind a word picture that would explode with meaning for this learned teacher of the Law.

"Just as Moses lifted up the snake in the desert," Jesus said in 3:14-15, "so the Son of Man must be lifted up, that everyone who believes in him may have eternal life." Then, to further explain that word picture, Jesus went on to say the often-quoted words, "For God so loved the world . . . "

A snake lifted high in the desert? What was Christ referring to? How would that word picture help Nicodemus understand who Jesus was and what He had come to do?

While we may struggle to connect the two verses, Nicodemus instantly would have seen Christ's allusion as a crystal-clear picture of who He was claiming to be. That's because this religious leader had surely studied Numbers 21:4-9 and the story of how many people were saved by looking up to a snake hung on a pole.

When the nation of Israel was wandering in the wilderness, the people began to grumble about Moses' leadership. They even questioned God's wisdom in leading them into the desert at all—and that's when they crossed the line.

God judged the critical Hebrews by sending fiery serpents among them. Once bitten, the individual would die, and that led to a massive cry from the people for Moses to plead with God for a way of escape. Moses did intercede on their behalf, and God gave him a most unusual remedy to their life-and-death dilemma.

Moses was directed to cast in bronze a likeness of the lethal snake. Then that bronze serpent was to be placed on one of the poles used to carry the tribal banners—a long pole with a crossbeam attached. Now, when any of the people were bitten by the deadly vipers, all they had to do was to look up at the serpent—on a cross—and they would be healed.

Look up at a snake on a cross and be healed? As simple as it sounds, I'm sure some people who were bitten by the snakes felt it was just too silly a request, or not complicated enough, or it didn't involve enough effort on their part. But as they soon learned all too well, those who put their faith in what God said and looked up would live, and all those who didn't would die.

Now can you understand the word picture behind the most familiar verse in the New Testament? Jesus was telling Nicodemus, "I'm like that snake Moses lifted up in the wilderness. Every person has been bitten by sin and will die, yet God has provided a way of escape. For when I take on the sins of the world—and become like that snake on the cross—those who look up to Me will be saved."

What clearer picture could Christ have given about our need for salvation and the only way of escape? Yet still today, there are those who think God's plan is too simple, not scientifically demonstrable, or doesn't involve enough human effort—and all those people stay poisoned by sin and chained to the terrible consequences, because they refuse to look in faith to Christ on the cross.

Whether it's the well-known word picture of a Good Shepherd or the powerful imagery of a bronze serpent, God has always shared bits of His character and personality through emotional word pictures. And those same pictures can also help us remember the truths of Scripture.

2. Word Pictures Help Us Understand and Remember the Truths of Scripture

How could the Infinite communicate His truths to finite human beings? The problem is similar—though on a much greater scale—to meeting with a doctor (perhaps a specialist) and having him explain your condition in technical terms. He's probably literally speaking Latin for all you know. Yet when he asks if you understand, you nod your head and say, "Mmm," knowingly. But inside you're thinking, *What was all that? Am I going to live another eighty years or die tomorrow?*

When it comes to understanding some of the great truths of the Bible, we can feel just like that. We know we're *supposed* to understand, so we look at each other and say, for instance, "Wow, isn't justification great?" But on the inside, we're as confused as if we were in that Latin-loving doctor's office.

God knew, however, that emotional word pictures can cut through the fog and help us understand His Word in a deeper, more intimate way. In fact, *God uses emotional word pictures to communicate almost all His most important truths.*

God consistently uses
emotional word pictures to communicate His
most important truths.

You may have heard your Sunday school teacher or a Bible college professor use the word *reconciliation* to describe one of the aspects of our relationship with Christ. But if you're like most of us, that word doesn't seem to have much personal impact.

Watch how Ephesians 2:14-15 makes that truth come alive, however. Talking about how Gentiles are now able to share a relationship with God that was once reserved for Jews, Paul said, "For he himself is our peace, who has made the two one and *has destroyed the barrier, the dividing wall of hostility.* . . . His purpose was to create in himself one new man out of the two, thus making peace" (italics ours).

What a powerful picture! For centuries, the Jews were privileged to be God's chosen people, standing on one side of a "wall" that separated them from the rest of humanity. To symbolize this separation, the Jews even built a literal wall around the inner and outer courts of the Temple, allowing only Jews to pass into the inner court, where God's presence dwelt in the Holy of Holies.

Try as the Gentile nations might, they could never find a battering ram big enough to break down that wall and become full participants with the Jews in God's blessings. But when Christ came, through His death and resurrection He tore down the dividing wall so that *everyone* could have a loving relationship with the Father.

Like East and West Germans celebrating the fall of the Berlin Wall, we realize through Paul's dramatic picture that something we once could not have (peace with God) is now ours for the taking. That's reconciliation, made clearer than any theological definition.

Our security as believers is also made clear by yet another word picture. In Ephesians 1:13 we read, "And you also were included in Christ when you heard the word of truth, the gospel of your salvation. Having believed, you were *marked in him with a seal,* the promised Holy Spirit" (italics ours).

In biblical times, when a king wanted to make sure his letter went undisturbed to its final destination, he poured a spot of molten candle wax on the end of the scroll, then stamped in his seal with a signet ring. The only way to open the letter was to break the seal. Thus the letter was safe, because any tampering would be obvious and would bring down the king's wrath.

What a picture of how God has provided "safe passage" for us who believe in Him! As New Testament believers, we can know we are sealed by the Holy Spirit and don't have to pray like David of old, "Do not . . . take your Holy Spirit from me."[5]

Even the book of Romans, held by many to be the jewel of Paul's theological teaching, is filled with word pictures. To explain how all are bound up in sin, both Jew and Gentile, he quoted a series of Old Testament word pictures: " 'There is no one who does good, not even one.' 'Their throats are open graves. . . .' 'The poison of vipers is on their lips.' "[6] Regarding our dedication to Christ, Paul wrote, we are to "offer your bodies as living sacrifices, holy and pleasing to God"[7] —that is, we're to lay our lives and talents on God's altar.

Throughout the Scriptures are moving word pictures that carry home God's truth and help us remember what's being taught. For example, try reading Isaiah 53 (the gripping picture of the suffering Messiah) without experiencing—and remembering—the emotions wrapped around the many word pictures there.

"He was led like a lamb to the slaughter, and as a sheep before her shearers is silent, so he did not open his mouth."[8] "We all, like sheep, have gone astray, . . . and the Lord has laid on him the iniquity of us all."[9]

Word pictures can draw us closer to God and bring more clarity to our knowledge of Him. Yet with the positive emotion word pictures carry, they're also a powerful tool God uses to bring us comfort and encouragement.

3. Word Pictures Are a Primary Way God Gives Us Hope and Encouragement

To see how word pictures can deepen our love for God and help us experience His love, there's no better place to turn than to the many prayers found in the Psalms.

When David was fleeing for his life from his son Absalom, for example, he prayed, "O Lord, how many are my foes! How many rise up against me! . . . But you are a shield around me, O Lord."[10]

On another occasion, David was celebrating his deliverance from Saul and praised God using a word picture: "The Lord is my rock, my fortress and my deliverer; my God is my rock, in whom I take refuge. He is my shield and the horn of my salvation, my stronghold."[11]

In our own lives, we've seen that using a word picture can help turn a stale prayer time into a meaningful conversation with God. For example, I (John) have often turned to Psalm 1 and used the word picture there as a pattern for prayer.

The psalm reads, "Blessed is the man who does not walk in the counsel of the wicked. . . . But his delight is in the law of the Lord. . . . He is like a tree planted by streams of water, which yields its fruit in season and whose leaf does not wither."[12] That picture can become a clearly guided prayer: "O Lord, I ask that You keep my feet in the path of wisdom today, and that You would send my roots deeper into You than ever before."

As for me (Gary), my entire life and view of prayer were changed through experiencing the word pictures Christ gave of the widow seeking protection, and of the man who woke his neighbor at night to get food for an unexpected guest.[13]

Besides being the tool that both David and Solomon used to express their fears, doubts, praise, and sorrow, word pictures are also one of the primary ways in which God ministers His love to us.

Pictures of Love, Hope, and Support

Have you ever gone through a difficult trial and doubted God cared for you or that He would protect you during that tough time? Listen to the word pictures God chose once to reassure us of His Love:

"He who dwells in the shelter of the Most High will rest in the shadow of the Almighty. I will say of the Lord, 'He is my refuge and my fortress, my God, in whom I trust.' Surely he will save you from the fowler's snare and from the deadly pestilence. He will cover you with his feathers, and under his wings you will find refuge; his faithfulness will be your shield and rampart."

Like a young child standing in her daddy's shadow, a soldier retreating to an armed fortress for cover, or a young eagle seeking the warmth of its mother's wings, we see in those encouraging words from Psalm 91:1-4 pictures of God's love and care for each of us.

Have you ever been so alone that you doubted even God was there? Let's look at a snapshot from a trip someone took centuries ago down the dimly lit road of doubt.

"Where can I go from your Spirit? Where can I flee from your presence? If I go up to the heavens, you are there; if I make my bed in the depths, you are there. If I rise on the wings of the dawn, if I settle on the far side of the sea, even there your hand will guide me."

Those reassuring words from Psalm 139:7-10 show us that no matter where we go or how lonely we feel, we can never lose God's presence or His ability to lead us through whatever situation we find ourselves in.

Have you wondered if God really deals with the Castros, Khadafis, and Saddam Husseins of the world? Gaze at this picture from the hand of the prophet Isaiah:

"Do you not know? Have you not heard? . . . He brings princes to naught and reduces the rulers of this world to nothing. No sooner are they planted, no sooner are they sown, no sooner do they take root in the ground, than he blows on them and they wither, and a whirlwind sweeps them away like chaff."[14]

Whether the issue is depth to our prayers, help for our doubt, or aid in our fears, Scripture uses word pictures time and again to bring comfort and encouragement.

Even on the last night of Christ's earthly life, He employed word pictures to make sure the disciples knew of His Father's care and provision for them. While they were in the Upper Room, not only did Jesus promise the presence of a great Counselor who would come alongside them, but He also told them, "In my Father's house are many rooms; if it were not so, I would have told you."[15]

So far, we've seen that word pictures can draw us closer to Christ, help us grasp and remember key biblical truths, and give us hope and encouragement. But one more fact stands out as an important reason for Christians to use them regularly. Just like Jesus, we need to be able to translate the gospel into a picture that can span even the greatest differences.

4. Word Pictures Provide a Powerful Tool for Evangelism

A welder used his welding tools as visual aids in helping a co-worker come to know Christ. Both men understood how important a good welding job would be on a key stress point of a building. By explaining about how Christ is the only one who can weld our lives together without having the seams come apart, the welder led his friend to the Lord.

An airplane mechanic used an "unsafe plane" illustration to confront a fellow worker with his sins and lead him to the Savior. Time and again, the everyday objects, stories, and remembrances drawn from the wells we write about in chapters 7-10 have been used for deeper communication between people—and between them and God.

Just ask those on the mission field how important it is to use word pictures in communicating spiritual truth. They'll tell you stories like Don Richardson's, which he captured in his exceptional book, *Peace Child.*[16]

Don was laboring among the Sawi tribe of Indonesia, struggling to communicate the gospel. Yet to this savage band, known for their human sacrifice and even cannibalism, he seemed to be going backward rather than forward.

They had accepted him warily into their midst because of the tools, medicine, and farming skills he brought, but they weren't interested in what he said about Jesus—until he told them about Judas.

When he recounted the story of Judas's betraying Christ around the tribal fire one night, suddenly the tribesmen became agitated and even cheered and shook their spears. Little did Don know that in their culture, treachery was admired. Tricking an enemy into thinking you were his friend—and then killing him—was considered one of the greatest warrior skills!

Don was totally frustrated that in all his months of labor, the only reaction he had gotten from these men was cheers for Judas, not praise for Jesus. But that's when God opened his eyes to an enormously effective word picture.

This culture had a custom Don had heard about. If war broke out between neighboring tribes, they had one sure way to restore peace. The chief of one tribe was to take a young child from among his people and give it to the chief of the opposing tribe. Then, as long as that child lived—*that peace child*—there would be a truce between the tribes.

At last, Don had his entry point into this culture that so needed Christ. And that night around the tribal fire, he told the natives about how God and all people struggle because of sin, and of the war inside them as a result. Then he told them about God's Peace Child—Jesus Christ—and how He lives forever to make peace between God and humanity.

In Don's stirring book, you can read about the evangelistic fervor that broke out in that tribe, and in neighboring tribes, when the people received a picture of God's love they could understand.

It's not only on the mission field that word pictures can help spread the good news, either. For years, Campus Crusade for Christ has used its "The Four Spiritual Laws" booklet as a witnessing tool, complete with drawings and even an explanation of the Christian life showing the "locomotive" of facts pulling the "caboose" of our feelings. This small tract, basically an extended word picture, has helped thousands find Christ.

From evangelism to discipleship, from encouragement to correction, word pictures help us strengthen our own spiritual lives. And perhaps as an added benefit, they can help us pass that life on to others.

As we close this chapter, we'd like to tell you about a final word picture used by one of the greatest preachers of all time. Charles Haddon Spurgeon died in 1892, but even now, one of the best compliments a preacher can get is for someone to say he preaches like Spurgeon.

While the printed messages of other great orators are gathering dust, Spurgeon's sermons are still read —and *preached*—today. And it should come as no surprise that his sermons were full of word pictures aimed at his listeners' hearts.

Several books of his works remain in print, but a story about him recounted on Paul Harvey's radio program just before one Easter is our personal favorite.

It seems that Spurgeon was struggling with his Easter sermon one year, and even as late as the Saturday before, he was walking the streets of London, trying to capture just the right phrases and illustrations.

That's when he saw a young boy walking by who was one of the city's many street children. This rough, ill-clothed lad was carrying an old, bent bird cage, and inside was a sorrowful-looking field sparrow.

Intrigued by the sight, Spurgeon stopped the boy and asked him about the bird.

"Oh, this?" the boy answered. "It's just a sparrow, and it's *my* bird. I found it."

"What are you going to do with it?" the great clergyman asked.

"Well—" the boy said. "I think I'll play with it for a while, and then when I'm tired of playing with it—I think I'll kill it." He made that last comment with a wicked grin.

Moved with compassion for the bird, Spurgeon asked, "How much would you sell me that bird for?"

"You don't want this bird, mister," the boy said with a chuckle. "It's just a bleeding field sparrow."

But when he saw the old gentleman was serious, suddenly his mind took a step toward extortion.

"You can have this bird for—two pounds." Two pounds at that time would be worth more than a hundred dollars today—an astronomical price for a bird worth only pennies. "That's my price. Take it or leave it," the boy said defiantly.

Spurgeon did pay the price, and then he took the bird to a nearby field and let it go. . . . But he wasn't finished with the cage.

The next morning, at the great Metropolitan Tabernacle where he preached, an empty bird cage sat on the pulpit as people took their seats.

"Let me tell you about this cage," Spurgeon said as he began the sermon he had stayed up late rewriting. Then he recounted the story about the little boy and how he had purchased the bird from him at a high cost.

"I tell you this story," he said, "because that's just what Jesus did for us. You see, an evil specter called Sin had us caged up and unable to escape. But then Jesus came up to Sin and said, 'What are you going to do with those people in that cage?'

"'These people?' Sin answered with a laugh. 'I'm going to teach them to hate each other. Then I'll play with them until I'm tired of them—and then I'll kill them.'

"'How much to by them back?' Jesus asked.

"With a sly grin, Sin said, 'You don't want these people, Jesus. They'll only hate You and spit on You. They'll even nail You to a cross. But if You do want to buy them, it'll cost You all Your tears and all Your blood—Your very life!'"

Spurgeon concluded, "That, ladies and gentlemen, is just what Jesus did for us on the cross. He paid the ultimate, immeasurable price for all who would believe, that we might be free from the inescapable penalty of death."

How about you? Has there been a time in your life when you responded to what Jesus did for you on the cross? Has there been a specific moment when you know you trusted Christ as the only way out of the cage of death?

Our prayer is that all who pick up this book will find the word pictures in Scripture to be a light to their path—a guiding light leading them out of the cage of death and into the wonderful freedom and everlasting life of a deep, personal relationship with Jesus Christ.

CAN
WORD
PICTURES
BE MISUSED?

CHAPTER SIXTEEN

The Dark Side of Emotional Word Pictures

We have devoted almost all of this book to the benefits of using emotional word pictures. Frankly, our heart's desire would be to quit right here, without looking beyond their positive side. But no matter how powerfully word pictures can launch emotional arrows right to a person's heart, they are powerless with certain people who seem to wear three-inch-thick, tungsten steel armor.

Not only will such people deflect word pictures—even those offering praise or encouragement—but they'll also often pick up the same arrow, turn it into a flaming dart, and shoot it back at us.

With all the power word pictures have for good, they also have an evil twin that can't be ignored. Mastering word pictures can be extremely advantageous to a relationship. But put in the wrong hands, they can be very dangerous.

As we began our historical research of emotional word pictures, we noticed a disturbing pattern. Namely, some of the most destructive people throughout the ages have, in large part, brought about that damage through word pictures.

Such individuals are often infamous for the human carnage they've caused. But some of the most damaging individuals we've known have never fired a gun or incited a riot. They've simply used the power of words to break down and destroy marriages, families, friendships, and businesses. These people may have never pulled the trigger. But their words have shoved a loaded gun into another person's hand, then pointed it at that person's temple.

Mastering word pictures can be extremely advantageous to a relationship. But put in the wrong hands. they can be very dangerous.

Without a doubt, the use and misuse of word pictures have shown us the absolute truth of the statement, "Life and death are in the power of the tongue."[1]

A faithful doctor tells a patient not only the advantages of taking a medication, but also explains its dangers and possible side effects. In like manner, we'd be remiss not to discuss the potential harm when the language of love is twisted into a language of hate.

At their best, word pictures share praise and correction, improve insight, and develop lasting intimacy and better understanding. They are at their worst when used to control, suppress, hurt, or manipulate others. We've labored diligently to convey the life-changing tool of emotional word pictures. But now we want to warn you. There may be those who will turn this tool against you and use it as a weapon.

The fact that some people can misuse a word

picture's innate power to affect lives should not deter us. A concerned husband can get behind the wheel of a car and rush his expectant wife to the hospital; but put an angry alcoholic behind the wheel, and you have a weapon that can kill.

We still drive cars, because of their power for good. But we are aware and cautious of their power to hurt and cripple. The same thing is true with emotional word pictures. We should be delighted to find a tool that can breathe new life into our communication and relationships. But in the wrong hands, like those of *der Führer,* Adolf Hitler, this tool can also convey words of death.

Words of Life, Words of Death

The years before World War II found Germany in troubled economic and political times. With its economy at a standstill, the elected government faced growing discontent from the working classes.

In that unsettled time, one man saw his chance for power. Hitler had grandiose ideas, but he needed a rallying point to gather a following. His restless mind had to find some symbol that could carry him into the spotlight for which he longed and lived.

An obscure man who was prone to fits of depression, he failed to enter the front doors of political power. But he opened wide the back door with a word picture, pulling his countrymen to himself and his radical views.

The twisted picture he painted was of the Jews, a race he described as "evil and slanderous"—a "corrupt" people who had "crept into Rhineland" and stolen the power and wealth from the German worker.[2] The word pictures he so insidiously crafted and so often used were then sold daily to the working class struggling to buy bread in long depression lines. In so doing, he spread unfounded anger and resentment in crowds of unemployed or underemployed workers. These fears and frustrations were like sparks on dry tinder. Hitler then gleefully fanned the flames into hatred. Listen to one of the hundreds of scathing denouncements he used to incite and inflame the nation:

> The Jewish race is a parasite living on the body and the productive worker of our nation. . . . Only when this Jewish virus infecting the life of the German people has been removed, can one hope to establish a co-operation between nations which shall be built upon a lasting understanding.

> The Jews are fond of saying, "Workers of the World Unite!" *Workers of all classes and of all nations, I tell you, wake up and recognize your common enemy!*[3] (Italics ours.)

With his symbol of hatred in hand, Hitler was surrounded by a growing legion of followers that shouted down any political or religious leaders who opposed him. The struggling German working class swallowed his reason for their economic and social distress. And the corrupt picture he painted of the Jews became the scapegoat for all Germany's problems.

Hitler's ability to twist people's minds and souls—especially the minds of the young—was, in large part, due to his skills as a communicator. Unfortunately, he's not the only one to wield negative power over others' lives. His evil clones and counterparts have marred every generation before and since. Take Jim Jones, for example.

Echoes of Evil

Have you ever wondered what Jones said to prompt hundreds of people to leave their country of birth and join in a death march to Guyana?

In the early days at his church in Los Angeles, his pulpit would rock with word picture after word picture.[4] He used them like chains to bind and enslave hundreds of men and women to his teachings. Listen to the picture-filled sermon he gave that later proved tragically prophetic:

> In my mind, we are at battle. We are a mass of people, so many that it actually dims the rising of the sun.
>
> And this mass is marching and singing. They have enemies who are ordered to fire on them. Their bodies are splintering into the sky. But the people keep coming and will not be stopped.[5]

His control over his followers was so powerful that more than nine hundred people followed Jones's words into darkness. They have not been the only ones to die. Charles Manson's followers did their share of killing. Like Jones, he, too, led a band of fanatical followers on a tirade of death. And he, too, was a master of word pictures.[6]

Cult leaders across time have drawn on mental pictures and mystical symbols, such as Satanists' upside-down cross, that are actually word pictures for their hidden teachings. The same is true of contemporary cults, which have adopted such religious symbols as the cross, rainbow, and oasis to promote their own brand of counterfeit Christianity.[7]

Political and cult leaders have long used word pictures to strangle physical and spiritual life from people. Tragically, there is a much less conspicuous group that does every bit as much damage: men and women who practice their destructive art from within regular homes in average neighborhoods. These people emotionally cripple, crush, and control their spouses and children. The more we read about and talk with them and their victims, the more we see that they, too, are masters of word pictures.

These are people who, in many ways, can't love back. And through their words, they actually endanger the physical, mental, emotional, and spiritual lives of others. Jackie's father is a perfect example.

A Case Study in Words That Control

Jackie grew up in a home that could more accurately be described as a nightmare. Because her family background was so damaging, it's no wonder she ended up in a psychiatric ward.

I (John) met her there years ago when I was in school. At the time, there was something about her I never could understand. I walked right past it then, but at the heart of her fears were two emotional word pictures. Each was a vivid image of cruelty and fear that helped cause her mental collapse and finally pushed her into darkness.

With an alcoholic father, fear and uncertainty were her constant companions. He had a nickname for her that he used constantly when he was drunk and angry: Demon Child. An on-again, off-again painter, her father was addicted to horror films and books, as well as alcohol. The lower he sank as a man, the more "manly" he felt by frightening his sensitive, impressionable daughter with horrible stories.

Most nights, with his cruel laugh chasing her down the hallway to bed, she would lie awake for hours. She was afraid to go to sleep, lest some of the horrible things he said were inside her body decided to come out. Even when she got older and professed she didn't believe in demons, she still couldn't shake the negative scars his word picture left on her self-image. Over the years, as she grew to a young woman, his words burned like sulfuric acid poured on her soul. And then one night, that pain was multiplied a hundredfold.

In a drunken fit, he barged into his daughter's bedroom and robbed her of what little remnants of innocence and childhood she had left. As if the incest wasn't bad enough, he left her a second, terrifying word picture on his way out.

As she lay in bed, fighting back tears of shame and pain, she was told that if she ever revealed to anyone what happened, a curse would be on her. He said the most horrible things would happen to her—perhaps a week or maybe even a year later if she violated their secret. But one night, she would wake up to the footsteps and then the clawing of someone outside her window, coming to get her—someone who would kill her in the most terrible way.

As a child, it never occurred to Jackie that her father was insane. And so, like many other times before, she choked down this latest dose of fear and shame. But she never closed her eyes until morning sunlight bathed each corner of her room.

Jackie did her best to go on with her life, and tried not to let her anguish show. Outwardly, she looked as peaceful as a cemetery, but a war was raging deep within. There seemed to be no place to rest, no place to hide. With no earthly source of comfort, she even tried praying. But as she knelt beside her bed, pouring out the terrible burden on her heart for the first time, she was suddenly overcome with fear.

In telling God her problems, had she just broken the

secret and loosed her father's curse? Would the stranger kill her? By night she was stalked by the thought of someone standing outside her window with a knife; by day, by the words, "Demon Child."

On the edge of sanity, she finally told her mother the terrible secret she had been hiding. For a moment, she felt relieved that her horrible burden had been shared with someone else. But then her mother suddenly slapped her and accused her of lying. That pushed her over the edge. Gobbling down a handful of sleeping pills, she sought shelter in the darkness of death.

She survived that first suicide attempt and stayed in a psychiatric ward for two months before returning home to her parents. But within six months, word reached me that she had taken her life. Jackie died a frightened child, more afraid of the dark side of her father than of death itself.

We realize Jackie's story is extreme. It's probably the most graphic example we know of the tongue's destructive power. While the damage in many homes is less life-threatening, there are severe emotional and physical tolls, nonetheless.

Everyday Examples of the Dark Side of Word Pictures

We know a salesman who can't keep a job, in large part, because he can't rise above his father's words from the past. They were spoken after the first and only baseball game his dad came to watch. He may have intended them to "motivate" his son to do better, but they had a dramatically different result.

"You're pathetic," he said, after his son struck out and made two errors in the two innings he played. "You're just a fourth-string player. Don't bother asking me to take off work again until you're first string.

In fact, don't bother asking me at all. *You'll always be fourth string."*

This certainly wasn't the only cutting thing his father ever said to him. He made a career of speaking damaging words. But the picture of being a "fourth-string" person has stayed with his son for years—the way all word pictures do. And now this grown man can never seem to be "first string" in anything—including as a husband and father.

But he isn't alone. We know a housewife whose mother repeatedly gave her the following word picture:

"Diane, when they're lowering me into my grave, then you'll be sorry you didn't come by more often to take me to the store and tell me what that husband of yours is doing. You'll be sorry you neglected me like a dog at the pound."

Every insensitive demand her mother made was punctuated by the guilt-causing sentence, "One day you'll be sorry, Diane, as they lower me into my grave." Her mother jerked her around like a kite on a string.

Even when Diane would stamp her foot down and try to stand her ground, she would slip into periods of anger and depression. If she didn't run to do some senseless errand for her mother, she would walk into days of terrible guilt for not "loving" her mother as she should.

"You're a bum!" "What an air-head!" "If your brains were gunpowder, you couldn't blow your nose!" Each of us is capable of occasionally saying negative things to our children or spouse that we would like to have back.

Such words, spoken in the heat of an argument, can hurt and punish. But over the years, the most damaging words we've seen aren't necessarily those that are spoken rashly. Rather, the most damaging ones carry a cold, hardened purpose and are used to manipulate, punish, and control.

But what kind of people gravitate to the dark side of word pictures? And why?

Before we express our feelings about the "whys" involved, let's look at the profile of "who" is involved —that person who can't love back and never seems to *hear* the word pictures we share. We're afraid this is the kind of man or woman who could take the communication tools found in this book and use them to emotionally crush others.

We don't claim that what follows is an exhaustive picture of such a person. But we have consistently seen a similar pattern emerge. If it can help you spot the misuse of word pictures, our warning will be well served.

Profile of a Person Who Consistently Uses the Dark Side of Word Pictures

In talking with a great many victims of hurtful homes, we've begun to see a common profile of the person who repeatedly shares hurt, not love. Often he can appear socially acceptable to others, but emotionally that person can be deadly to live with.

In all, we've seen five characteristics of those who twist word pictures into weapons for destruction. Before we look at this list, let us mention again that we are all capable of saying damaging things. To a degree, we may periodically see ourselves in each of these categories. But to persistently find ourselves (or someone else) practicing them as a lifestyle—or to adamantly deny they apply—should raise the warning flag that there may be danger ahead.

* * *

The Dark Side of Emotional Word Pictures

People who consistently use the dark side of word pictures jump on your faults but fight off any correction you give them.

At the heart of a person who would use words to punish others is a terrible need to keep the light of correction shining on someone else, not turned toward him- or herself. People who tend to be the most destructive with their words are lightning-quick to see the faults of others. But they move at a glacier's pace when it comes to accepting any personal fault or problems in their own lives.

These laser-quick faultfinders rarely demonstrate their destructive talent on outsiders. Their skill is saved for use on those at home. As a result, the near-perfect image they present to those passing the house can confuse and torment those who live within. They can begin thinking that perhaps their home is actually "normal" and that they should be more happy and secure.

Such a person uses word pictures as weapons to constantly correct someone else, but you won't see him using them for praise. If you should dare to correct him, you'll meet the fury of a cornered snake. For if he gave one inch, by accepting one of your word pictures for correction, it would unlock miles of litter-strewn roadways in his life.

People who consistently use the dark side of word pictures often make you feel terrible with their words, and somehow convince you it's your fault.

There is something remarkably consistent about people who misuse word pictures. They are somehow able to slide in the blade of hurtful words and then retract it without ever leaving evidence to incriminate themselves.

For example, take the man's father who called him a

"fourth-string" person. We confronted him with his persistent, negative word picture, and he explained it away as a positive, motivating factor in his son's life.

"Years ago, the best coach I ever had told me the same thing! He told me I'd never be better than fourth string, and I went out and proved him wrong. That's all I want for my son. I know he can do it. I just want him to finally prove to his family and friends that he's a success!"

Sounds pretty good. But not if you press his words. While the veneer might look as solid as oak, his imbedded barbs are as rotten as soaking driftwood. Somehow, when his "fourth-string" speeches were communicated over the years, they didn't carry the altruistic meaning he claimed. Instead, his words made an incision that was so quick and clean, it left his son wondering why he carried around so many emotional scars.

His paltry explanation did something else to his son. It left him hating himself for being overly sensitive, when all his father was trying to do was help him. This poor "fourth-string" son never saw the fire behind his father's words, but wisps of smoke often stung his eyes. Not only did his father refuse to see any fault in his own behavior, but he was an expert at hurting his son—and making him think it was his own fault.

People who misuse word pictures often do so to accomplish a good thing in a bad way. But because they always have the other person's "best interest" in mind, it excuses the emotional knife-marks left in their victims.

People who consistently use the dark side of word pictures often cover a trio of personal problems with words of darkness.

At the heart of most addictions—whether it be to sex, alcohol, drugs, or verbally hurting others—is a trio of personal problems.[8] Namely, fear, anger, and loneliness. It's hard to get a destructive person to come in for counseling. After all, they don't feel the need.

People who are addicted to hurting others include men and women who carry so many personal problems that they're uncomfortable with the warmth of a close relationship. Like a prisoner locked in a dungeon for months who cringes at his first glance at raw sunlight, they stay in the shadows. They are more familiar with speaking and hearing words of darkness than words of light, which make them feel out of place.

People who are filled with pictures of fear and anger, covered with deep-seated loneliness, are prime candidates to misuse word pictures. With their words, they re-create for others their own terrible world of darkness.

People who consistently use the dark side of word pictures often lack the skills of empathy and encouragement.

The housewife's mother who consistently used guilt to motivate her daughter had another characteristic common to those who misuse word pictures. She demanded instant empathy, understanding, and encouragement from her daughter, but was unable to give these things in return.

She wanted her needs met—now! But never once did she see the toll it took on her daughter's marriage to drop everything and rush to meet a petty need. Such needs included getting her an extra half gallon of milk just before her daughter went out of town for the weekend. ("After all, the weekend is coming, and you know I can't get out to the stores myself, and they're all so busy anyway, and you're not going to be here for days, and . . .")

Watch out for those who demand empathy for themselves, but who can never see the glaring needs for comfort and encouragement in your life. As with this punishing mother, they can latch hold of a word picture and use it to control, manipulate, and enslave.

People who consistently use the dark side of word pictures often don't respect legitimate boundaries around your life.

As with anyone who commits incest, Jackie's father smashed down the healthy boundaries between parent and child. He would not only walk into her room unannounced or interrupt her conversations at any time, but he also respected no boundary to her person as well.

This father is a dramatic example (although not an uncommon one, unfortunately) of those who destroy protective fences. Such people often use word pictures to erase any barriers they feel separate them from smothering another person.

The housewife's mother would destroy her daughter's marriage because it represented a fence between her and getting her selfish needs met. And Jackie's father wouldn't even allow the natural barrier of sexual protection to stand in his home.

If you awaken to a word picture crashing down on you, the blow is often inflicted by someone who wants to destroy a perceived boundary between you and them, no matter how healthy it might be.

These five characteristics are the most common and most destructive ways we see word pictures being misused. Please let them be a warning. For the damage that we or someone else may cause can last a lifetime.

A great concern of ours is that people will take this list and go off on a witch hunt. That is certainly not our intent. All of us can be less encouraging than we should be, less open to correction, less sensitive. Yet, if a person has all of these characteristics and manifests them consistently, don't expect to make tremendous headway in confronting them. Do expect them to turn the power of word pictures against you. And do expect them to seek unhealthy control over your life and the lives of others.

After the Darkness Comes the Day

In the society and world we live in, there will come a time when we run into evil people. If this chapter succeeds in warning you of the negative power of their words and word pictures, then our purpose has been met. If it's done nothing but scare you away from using word pictures, we've missed our mark.

In C. S. Lewis's excellent children's series, *The Chronicles of Narnia,* his main character is a magnificent lion named Aslan. In one of the stories, this mighty lion befriends several children.

Two of them have already met Aslan, and the third is about to, but is fearful of the result:

"Is he—quite safe?" Susan asked. "'Course he isn't safe. But he's good," said Mr. Beaver."[9]

That's the way we feel about word pictures. History and experience have shown us that they are too powerful to be tame or safe. But they can be used for good.

We don't want to close the book on a negative note—and we won't. For there is warmth, love, and life that can come from our words and word pictures.

In the next chapter, we've personally chosen more than one hundred of the most powerful word pictures we've heard to share with you. Each may be used in your family, business, or friendships . . . or to stimulate your creativity in designing your own.

A TREASURY OF
WORD
PICTURES
AT YOUR
FINGERTIPS

CHAPTER SEVENTEEN

101 Life-Tested Word Pictures

Researching this book has been a particular joy. In large part, that's because it has involved sitting down over coffee with various couples or staying long after a conference has ended to talk with someone. In many everyday encounters and by letter, people have expressed to us that word pictures have made a very real difference in their lives.

We wish we could include the several thousand word pictures we've been fortunate enough to gather over the years. They're a collection of irrepressible gladness and inconsolable sadness. They're the words of an aged father writing a "blessing" to each of his children and the grief expressed by a grandmother who was far too busy for her children when they were young. They come from a husband who, for the first time, found the words to praise his wife, and from a wife who wrote the book on encouragement.

We've also gathered hundreds of word pictures—springing from business, family times, friendships, and spiritual life—that can challenge a person to think deeply about his or her relationships. We've been moved to tears in reading one word picture, and have erupted in laughter at another. They show the finest qualities of human character and all its frailties.

We hope you've enjoyed learning about this everyday concept with its extraordinary capacity to change lives. And we hope you'll be further encouraged by the sample of word pictures we've selected in the pages that follow.

In closing, we hope to hear from you about a word picture that has made a positive difference in your life. You've been given a powerful tool, and we'd love to know how it has been used for good. What's more, we'd like to leave you with a word picture of our own. It represents our deepest desires and brightest hopes that this communication concept will enrich your life and most important relationships:

Like the finest apple trees in the land, may all your relationships grow and prosper and bring forth much good fruit. May you stay planted beside life-giving springs of water, and may your blossoms bring forth a fragrance of love and encouragement to others. May God shelter you from storms and keep you forever in His sunlight.

Gary Smalley

John Trent

Today's Family
P.O. Box 22111
Phoenix, AZ 85028

Capturing the Joys and Struggles of Marriage

The Joys . . .

1. My husband treats me like a roomful of priceless antiques. He walks in, picks me up, and holds me with great care and tenderness. I often feel like I'm the most precious thing in our home. He saves the best hours and his best effort for me, not the television.

2. With the kind of job I'm in, I often feel like I'm walking on a desert trail on a hot, summer day. After struggling through the heat and cactus all day, I come to the end of a path and there's a beautiful pool of cool water. At last I'm at a place where I can drink and be refreshed. That's what it's like being with my wife. In forty-four years of marriage, I still feel that being with her is like coming upon an oasis.

3. I'm a ship with brightly painted banners riding the warm, gentle, Caribbean breeze of my husband's love. All through my childhood, I was forced into an unsafe ship and made to ride across the North Atlantic. I was nearly shipwrecked more times than I could count. But with my husband's love, I feel like I've traded ships and sailed around the world. Instead of the fierce gales of the Atlantic, I feel like there's always a steady warm trade wind blowing me to a safe harbor.

4. I felt like an acorn that was tossed into a pile of rocks. I never had the right amount of light or the proper soil, and so I grew into an oak tree that was bent and crooked. But in nine years of marriage, I feel that you've done the impossible. You've transplanted me to a place in the sun where I can at last grow straight and tall.

5. There have been times over the years when I've faced hailstorms that I thought would turn into tornadoes. But like the shelter of a storm cellar, I can always run to my husband to protect me from hardship. He's

as solid as a rock, and I know he'll always be there when the storm clouds blow into my life.

6. I feel like the kids and I are a valuable piece of farmland with dark, rich soil that would quickly become overgrown with brambles and thorns if it weren't cared for properly. Fortunately, my wife is like a master gardener. Every day, in many ways, she lovingly nurtures and cares for me. Primarily because of her skills at planting and raising an intimate relationship, we've got a garden that's the envy of all our neighbors.

7. I love my husband because he always makes sure I know I'm the number one woman in his life. He reminds me of a beautiful English setter. His amber coat glows as he romps in the meadow near our house. I know there are other dogs in the meadow—beautiful show dogs, far prettier than I. But he always ignores them and comes back to me. His soft brown eyes tell me each night, "There is no one but you."

8. When I turned thirty and was feeling insecure, my husband gave me just the word picture I needed. When he found me pouting and feeling afraid that he would leave me for another woman, he told me, "Sweetheart, when you live with a brand-new, gleaming white Cadillac convertible, there's no desire to rush out and drive a Volkswagen."

9. For me, life is sometimes like waterskiing. The towline is unexpectedly jerked, and I fall headlong. I try it again, only to be dumped once more and left in the water, shivering, exhausted, and alone. Just when I'm ready to give up, my wife lovingly speeds to my rescue. In an instant, she throws out a life line, and I pull myself from the water's icy grip. With her, I am warm, safe, and loved. My wonderful wife has rescued me again!

10. Before I lost my leg in an accident, I felt like any

other apple in a barrel. But for a long time after my surgery, I felt like I was rotten inside and out, and totally worthless to anybody else. Yet, my wife has never viewed me any differently. She knows I don't look like everyone else on the outside, but on the inside I've never changed. To her I am unique and complete.

11. My wife's love is like a huge glass of ice tea on a hot summer day. It's cool and crisp and its refreshment restores my strength and quenches the thirst of my dry, dusty soul.

12. My wife and I are like an all-star baseball team. I'm able to field some of the hard-hit grounders, and sometimes I knock the ball over the fence. But if it weren't for her consistency in stepping up to the plate day after day, we wouldn't have a winning season.

13. When I met you, I felt a rush of excitement ten times greater than when the first client walked into my office. We've been married for eight years now, and I've got many clients I get to spend time with. But spending time with you is still the most valuable appointment that goes into my book.

14. I feel like a happy little fox that was running through the woods one day and met a nice male fox. We fell in love, and he's become my closest companion. Despite occasional brushes with hunters and bigger animals, he always protects me. Even when it means standing up to fight for me, he takes on everything that's faced us. In a few months, we'll have a baby fox to care for. My prayer is that that little fox will grow to love his or her dad as much as I do.

15. Life's problems sometimes make me feel like the captain of a sinking ship. Often, the closer the ship gets to going under, the more those around me dive overboard and leave me to save the vessel by myself. I'm thankful to have a first mate who stays by my side

no matter what. If it weren't for her and the quiet, gentle strength she always uses to encourage me, I would have given up and jumped overboard a long time ago.

16. When I come home from work, I often feel like a fighter pilot whose jet has been riddled with bullets. It's so great to come home to my wife! Like a dedicated ground crew, she works overtime to bring me back to full strength and gets me ready to soar into battle again. I couldn't do it without her.

The Struggles . . .

17. Sometimes I feel like our miniature poodle. She was once the object of our deepest affection, but now she gets pushed aside. She continually seeks our love but to no avail. Just sitting near us would make her happy, but she's often sent in the other room by herself. I continually seek my husband's love, yet he pushes me away. I wish I could get some attention or even an occasional snuggle.

18. When I was first married, I felt like a beautiful, handcrafted, leather-bound, gold-trimmed book that had been presented to my husband as a gift from God. At first I was received with great enthusiasm and excitement—cherished, talked about, shared with others, and handled with care. As time has gone by, I've been put on the bookshelf to collect dust. Once in a while he remembers I'm here. But if only he would take me off the shelf and open me up! If only he'd see how much more I have to offer him!

19. I feel like a little boy's beloved dog. For seven months of the year, he takes wonderful care of me. We play, take long walks together, and shower one another with affection. But when the baseball season starts, he leaves me to play with his friends. He sometimes forgets to feed me and rarely has time for me. He's so

busy that he gives me just enough food, water, and attention to make me yearn for more. The sheen in my fur and spring in my step go away, and I dream about how wonderful it will be to have him back again. I just hope I can wait.

20. I know I can be a roaring flame of enthusiasm, but my wife often hoses me off with her words, and I wind up a dying ember. If she would only fan the fire with some encouraging words or a tender hug when I get home from work, I'd burn as brightly as ever.

Expressing the Joys and Challenges of Parenting

The Joys . . .

21. When I see my daughters and how well they're doing in life, pride swells within me like the snow-capped Rockies above a beautiful mountain valley. It's a feeling like I'm on top of the world. My children have moved away now, and most of the time the mountains stand at quite a distance. Yet, even from afar, looking at them fills me with wonder and thankfulness.

22. Experiencing my daughter's birth was like God leading me to a beautiful sandy beach and showing me an ocean full of future blessings that my daughter will bring. It's all been too wonderful to comprehend, too beautiful to believe.

23. My children are like stars in a desert sky. Each has a brilliance all its own and a unique place in creation. Like those stars, my children glimmer in their own special way and burn brightly with love for others. I hope that for as long as they live they will shine with the love I see now.

24. When my children go out of their way to call and come by, it's like getting an unexpected gift. You expect a present at Christmas. But nearly every week,

I get a card, a call, or a visit from one of my children. It's like getting Christmas presents all year long.

25. I feel like a nesting hawk, carefully feeding and protecting my children. With a keen eye and fine-tuned senses, I gather food and watch carefully for predators who seek to get at them. Tiring at times? Sure. Yet, I've never felt more important and useful. I cherish the demands of guarding and loving them.

26. When I come home from a busy day, I often feel like a woman stranded in a barren desert. Exhausted and thirsty, I long for a quiet, cool, peaceful oasis. My husband and son give me that place of rest and refreshment I need so much, by both their pleasurable company and their sacrificial willingness to help with duties around the home. I feel like I have two angels that are also my great friends, good helpers, and loving encouragers.

27. I love my family. When life makes me feel like I'm trying to bail out a sinking ocean liner with a paper cup, they lovingly pitch in and help. That doesn't decrease the amount of water pouring into the ship, but it sure helps get it out faster! I don't know how I ever lived without them!

28. My family is like a soft, overstuffed recliner, complete with every option and extra the manufacturer has ever made. Their words are warm and soothing like a heating element; their hugs like massagers that ease the aches and pains of life. With them around, I can tip way back but never fall to the ground. After spending time in my recliner, I've got the rest and loving support to keep going. My family is like a soft cushion of love.

29. Because of my children's constant affirmation, I feel like a beautiful, well-groomed show horse. My coat shines and my beautiful mane dances as I parade about. I often go out for a run with other show horses, and many of them feel abused and misused by their

children. I'm so thankful for the kids I've got, and the way they reflect even more love than I give them.

The Challenges . . .

30. For years when my son was young, my life was like spending a wonderful time in the quiet waters of a nearby beach. But lately, I feel like there has been a storm that caused the waves to pound the sand with boiling anger. I've been desperately searching for gentle swells and a safe place to swim. But if I'm not careful, no matter what subject I share with him or what I say, I get smashed by the waves and dragged out to sea. I'm so confused. I wish the storm would go away and we could get back to the quiet waters of friendship and respect we once had.

31. When I begin a difficult day at work, I feel as if I'm building a pyramid of dominoes. Early in the day, I'm able to stack the base securely and begin building. As the day progresses, the pyramid gets higher and more difficult to build. Yet, I'm able to keep it from falling. Finally, I get to the end of the day without tipping any of them over! But the moment I arrive home, one small problem with my children seems to topple the whole stack. I'm ashamed to admit it, but seeing my day falling around me makes me feel like not even coming home.

32. I feel like I'm a book in my father's office library. We are always admired but almost never read. Occasionally we're used as paperweights or to prop open a door. But day after day, I mainly sit on the shelf, my pages yellowing and cracked, my binding coming undone. I need my father to do more than just admire me at a distance. I need him to take me off the shelf and to see what's inside me. He's never taken the time to turn the pages and really get to know me. And that hurts so much.

33. Sometimes I feel like a teddy bear. My family

hugs me, tells me they love me, and always comment on how much fun I am to squeeze (I'm a little overweight). I love being hugged, but I can't seem to verbalize my love back to them. I was raised with so much criticism. Maybe it's my personality or the pressures at work that make it hard to say I love them. Maybe it's time for some changes.

34. I feel like a bear that's a month overdue for hibernation. I yawn and wrestle with waves of slumber sweeping over me. I want to crawl inside a nice, warm den and sleep for the rest of the season. But I can't because my newborn cubs aren't ready to hibernate, and I must watch them. If only they'd lie down and hibernate for a week—or even for a few hours—so that I could get some rest!

Telling Someone How I Feel Today

I'm Feeling Great . . .

·35. Today, I feel like a path that seems to be straightening out. The brilliant sunlight shines down on it, making the way sharp, clear, and easy to follow. There is more direction and definition to the path than there has been in years, and fewer rocks to climb over.

36. I feel like a tree branching out in every direction —sometimes uncontrolled, at other times graceful and elegant. Though my branches sag on occasion, they are full of dense, bright foliage. I've even learned to rejoice when my branches must be pruned. I've found that while it may be painful, God is always a tender, compassionate gardener. He prunes me not out of spite, but so I'll grow and see how much I can count on Him in any situation. I'm thrilled because I feel my roots of faith growing deeper every day!

37. I feel like a green tree progressing through the

seasons. Winter sometimes brings cold, harsh people who hurt me. But spring always returns, and with it comes new green leaves. I keep growing!

38. At work lately, I feel like a brightly decorated Christmas tree that gets tons of praise and encouraging comments on Christmas Day. Losing the forty pounds was worth all the work it took!

39. I used to feel like a valuable old chair that was scratched and painted numerous times, and then abandoned in a garage. But wonderfully, God has stripped off the old paint, polished and cared for me, and put me in a special place in His living room. He has given me life again!

40. I feel like a salmon fighting its way upstream, with an occasional stop in a calm eddy of friendship. Those cool waters always refresh me for the next part of my journey into the mainstream of life. With these pools of friendship along the way, I know I can continue to swim for as long as I have to.

41. I feel like I'm living in the country during springtime. The air is fresh, the buds are blooming, the meadowlarks are singing, and I feel great!

42. I feel like a helpless caterpillar, cut and bruised from the pain of life, but I've finally been wrapped in a healing cocoon of love. I can already tell that the wings of a monarch butterfly are beginning to emerge. Soon I'll be healed and more beautiful than ever. I can't wait!

43. I feel like a car. I'm a good basic model but I don't really have many extras. I know that some cars have more flash, but I know I don't need that. I'm sturdy and dependable, and it's great knowing I'm unique!

44. I feel like a beautiful old car that was in need of repair. An expert mechanic has been working to correct the problems. Though much of the work has

been painful, I can tell the car rides better already! Change is never easy, but I feel that my time in counseling has helped rebuild my engine and get me back on the road.

45. This conference has made me feel like an empty barrel that's now full of crystal-clear water after a much-needed spring rain. Many people around me need this water to refresh them, and finally I'm ready to give it to them!

46. As I reflect on my seventieth birthday, my travel through life has been like a trip to a faraway land. It's been full of excitement and uncertainty, which is sometimes scary but never boring. Through it all, I've met many new, interesting people and seen God's faithfulness displayed in ways I never thought possible. I've had a great life!

47. I've just seen an amazing miracle in my dad's life. For years, he's been too busy to spend any time with us kids or his grandchildren. But now that's all changed. Whenever I see him holding my son, I feel like I'm riding on Space Mountain at Disneyland! It's a little scary, but it's so exciting, I hope the ride never ends!

48. I feel like a beautiful Clydesdale horse, strong and powerful. I've been carefully cared for and nurtured since birth, and now I'm fully grown and ready to hitch up to life's challenges. I know my parents have equipped me to handle the heavy loads that are going to come in college, and I feel I'm up to the task.

49. I was born with a physical handicap, and when people express doubts about my ability to do something, I feel like a bumblebee. They look at me and say, "Aerodynamically, there's no way you can fly!" But my parents look at me and say, "The way you were made, you can't help but fly!" I've been buzzing around ever since!

50. I feel like a quaint log cabin nestled snugly in a forest that's blanketed by a carpet of silent, virgin snow. A stream gently bubbles its way through the woods, guided by the delicate silver moonbeams of a starlit winter sky. A warm fire glows within, its gentle plume rising into the calm stillness of the night air. I am content and at peace with all around me.

51. A special teacher in my life has taken me from being an ugly duckling to an elegant swan. She saw in me potential I didn't know was there, and patiently encouraged me when all others had given up. Now I swim in life's waters without fear. Thanks to her, I never lose what I have become even though things are turbulent at times.

52. Today I feel like a sunrise. As I pop up over the horizon and cast my light on the land, I'm excited about what the day will bring. As I ride the sky, life explodes in a flurry of activity, and I beam with the challenge ahead. I'm so worn out by evening that I let the moon take over so I can get some sleep!

53. I feel like a glass-smooth lake, reflecting the morning's glory. All around me, life is occurring just as it should. Hundreds of birds rise from their roosts, calling to each other about another day's flight. A beaver begins his busy day, preparing for the winter that lies ahead. And a doe with her gangly-legged fawn bows gently to the water's edge and drinks in quiet, cool refreshment. All my life I've been too busy to enjoy any of these beautiful things going on around me. Finally, I'm at peace with myself and can enjoy life's beauty.

54. I feel like the guy on the doughnut commercial. With working and taking care of three kids, it's always "time to make the doughnuts." But there's still nothing as sweet as doing just what I'm doing!

55. I just got back from vacation, and instead of

feeling like a horse pulling a cart, I feel like I'm a sleek jet—like those in the movie *Top Gun*. My engines are running all out, and I'm climbing to new heights and challenges. As I speed above the clouds, life suddenly seems more simple and more in focus. I can see for hundreds of miles. After only two weeks off, I feel like I'm soaring over those things that seemed so insurmountable when I was stuck on the ground, pulling a cart. I think I've convinced myself I need to take some more time off!

I'm Struggling . . .

56. I feel like a hamster in a maze of hills and dark holes, weary from wrong turns and dead ends. I'm scared I may never make it to the light. People sometimes look down to watch what I'm doing. Some encourage me; others make fun of my plight. I often do tricks to try and amuse them, but I'm always afraid of being rejected. And I never ever feel like I'm one of them.

57. I feel my life is as boring as a VCR tape on constant rewind—the same thing gets played over and over again. At times like that, I want to fast forward to the end and put in a tape with a new job, new house, and new car.

58. One day, I feel like I'm alone on a desert road, with nothing in sight. The next day, I'm on a beautiful path that's lined with trees, flowers, and grass. The sun is shining. It's beautiful! I'm torn between these two feelings—of contentment with being single and still wanting to be married. At times, I really do feel fulfilled, and I enjoy my life as a single. But the very next day, it's as if I'm in an endless desert with no hope that someone will rescue me.

59. As a single, I often feel like I'm standing outside a warm, cozy house full of my married friends who are laughing and enjoying one another. I feel cold and

alone. It's not that they won't let me in. I know it's me who has put the lock on the door, not them.

Telling Others How Much They Mean to Me

60. Returning home to you from a trip is like taking a quiet drive in the country after having driven a taxi in New York City for a week. No one is cutting me off or yelling at me. There are no red lights to frustrate me nor any crummy drivers to swerve into my path. Coming home is like driving on a country road where people actually wave because they like me and are glad to see me, not because they're mad.

61. Marrying you was like getting a release from life's prison of loneliness. For thirty-six years, I spent every night in solitary confinement. I now spend each night in a garden of love, with the one I love sleeping next to me.

62. You're as beautiful and delicate to me as the most expensive piece of Waterford crystal. Looking at you is like looking at a work of art, skillfully crafted by masters. Your every facet is unique and perfect in its own way. You sparkle in a rainbow of light, and every day I catch a new reflection of why I love you so much.

63. Being with you is as fulfilling as the first and only time I received a standing ovation from a class of students. As a teacher, I work so hard and rarely get any praise. But when that class showed its genuine appreciation by standing to applaud, it made all the work and long hours seem worthwhile. Honey, your encouragement and loving words make me feel like I come home to a standing ovation. Even when I haven't put in the time and don't deserve it, you support me like the best class I've ever had.

64. Your love is to me what going to McDonald's is to the kids—especially when they get to order all the chocolate shakes and French fries they can eat!

65. Your quiet, gentle spirit is like a delicate, beautiful flower. Sometimes, I get frustrated when you don't open up and share your feelings with me. But I've learned that if I'm patient and wait until you're ready, you'll bloom and share with me in a beautiful way.

66. My marriage is a lot like a raft trip. There are times when I take us down an uncharted section of the river, and we overturn and everything gets soaked. But I never see you complain. I know I tend to go off on a new idea without looking at a map, but you never hold it against me. I know I'm blessed to have you.

67. Though I'm just like millions of other women, when I'm with you I feel like a prize painting hanging in a place of honor in a lovely mansion. I'm the object of your undivided attention and the admiration of all who enter the room—all because you treat me like a priceless work of art.

68. Your love, so solid and enduring, is like a mountain rising out of the plains. I can always look to it, receive comfort from its presence, and know it will always be there. Its beauty moves me. And it's a monument to how much I love you!

69. When I woke up this morning, I got to thinking about your love being like a snowflake. It's gentle, soft, and unique in its every expression. And like an evening snowfall, your love blankets me when I awaken.

70. When I think of our marriage, I feel like Cinderella. Never in my wildest dreams did I think you'd ever want me. Yet, the slipper fit. And life with you, my Prince Charming, has been all I envisioned in my little-girl dreams!

71. My husband's love is like a huge ice cream sundae, *without the calories!* It is sweet and pleasing, and no matter how much I want, there's always more than enough!

Conveying Thoughts on Friends and Relationships

72. When I'm with my friends, I think about the time I climbed Mt. McKinley. I would have never made it to the top of that peak without the help of other climbers. In the same way, I thank God for the mountaintop friendships I have. They have helped me so much!

73. When I'm with you, I feel like I'm sleeping on a warm, comfortable waterbed. I can rest at night, always knowing that you'll be there for me. Your understanding gently rocks me to sleep, and the time I spend with you always leaves me refreshed and ready for a new day.

74. My friend is like a charming easy chair with big soft cushions. I'm always comfortable and secure with her. She's there for me whenever I need her. I know I can relax, take my shoes off, lean back, and just enjoy being with her. I'm so thankful for such a wonderful friend!

75. Dating you is like wearing designer jeans. Your label makes me really proud to be with you. You're such a quality person! And I don't even have to take you to the cleaners!

76. The surprise party you gave made me feel like a movie star who was recognized by a group of fans at the mall. It's a little uncomfortable to be surprised and to be the center of so much attention. But it also feels great!

77. The other day, I felt like a puppy at a pet store—admired by all, cared for by none. I wanted so much for someone to hold me and spend time playing with me. And then you stopped and sat down with me, even though you were way too busy to do so. Thanks for taking the time to love and care for me.

78. My friends and I are like a circus of happy clowns. We do some of the craziest things! We perform

so people can enjoy life's all-too-rare moments of laughter. What's unique about us is that when the performance is over, we can take off our masks and accept each other for who we really are. These guys are true friends; I hope we're together for a lifetime!

79. I've got a special friend who acts like a flashlight to me. When I'm lost or in the dark, sure enough—I see his light, piercing through the darkness, coming toward me. Then he leads me home to safety. At times, he even points his light on a problem area in my life that I've been trying to keep in the dark. I've learned to appreciate that.

80. I have a special friend who has an amazing ability to help me overcome my faults. She's like a skilled surgeon, with a keen eye for diagnoses and a sharp mind to wisely discern how best to solve the problem. When it's time for surgery, she soothes the pain with an anesthetic of genuine love and concern. Then, when the surgery is over, she gently closes the wound with tender stitches of compassion. But what I like about her the most is that, like any good surgeon, she constantly checks up on my progress and assures me I'll be better because of the operation.

81. The four of us are like a beautiful set of clothes. Each of us, by him- or herself, isn't that glamorous. Yet, God has styled us in such a way that people who see us together admire our beauty and style.

82. When I'm with my friends, I feel like we're on a giant surfboard together, riding the waves of Oahu's north shore. Sometimes the ride gets rough, but we're there to help each other stay aboard. We often catch a great wave and enjoy the thrill of riding it together. When one of us falls off, we all dive in after him. We really care about one another, and it's great to know that even if a shark attacks, someone will be on hand for the rescue.

83. I feel like a seed that contains every God-given

ingredient needed to grow. Yet, I'm dependent on others to provide the water, soil, and sunshine so I can sprout and develop. It's been so long since anyone provided me with the help I need that I'm a little afraid to trust others. But I'm not going to give up. I know that one day I'll find some friends here at school who can help me grow.

84. I feel a lot like an old sewing machine. I've been faithfully running for years, but I'm not as fast as I used to be. I squeak more often these days. That's why it's such a blessing to have friends who give me the oil of encouragement and support. With them, I know I have many years of faithful service left!

85. I'm like a mirror, trying to reflect God's image to others. Sometimes that's hard to do. It's so wonderful to have friends who will still love me in spite of my cracks!

Telling Others That I'm Hurting

86. I feel like a carpet that no one notices. I wish people would take off their shoes and appreciate my plush, soft comfort, but they don't. Instead, I get stomped on and ignored.

87. I feel like a computer operator who has spent months devising a special program, only to have the night janitorial crew accidentally pull the plug and lose my work. I've spent six months trying to design a great relationship with my girlfriend, only to find that someone else has taken her and pulled the plug on us. It's going to take a long time for the hurt to go away and to reprogram new friendships.

88. I feel like a daisy transplanted in a vast field of Texas bluebonnets. Those who admire the field don't realize I'm different. Before this, I was plucked from the ground, placed in a pot for a while, and then planted again. I'm now wilting for lack of water and

care, and no one hears my cries for help. Others' roots choke out any chance I have to grow again. Will anyone help me?

Expressing How I Feel About My Job

I Feel Great About What I'm Doing . . .

89. Our company is like the heavyweight champion of the world. Thousands of contenders are trying to knock us off. We're a bit like Rocky and Apollo Creed. It's between rounds; we're in the corner. We're bruised, battered, and bloodied. But we're going to stay in the ring. We're not going to give up. We're still going to be champions when this is over. No matter whom we face, we will never, never, never give up!

90. I feel like a hunting falcon. My company has trained me well. My skills have been honed razor-sharp. I have total confidence I can do a good job. Let me at 'em!

91. I'm like a baseball team in late September that has a great chance for the playoffs. I've had ups and downs this season, but things are looking good right now. I've gotten my second wind, and I'm going for it!

92. My boss made me feel great yesterday. He compared me to the center on a football team. It's not the flashiest position, but it's just as important as the others. In fact, much of the company's success depends on the center getting the ball to the quarterback. I'd never thought about it, but as the office manager I'm in the middle of the action. The plays all start with me. He said I deserve as much credit as the quarterback for the team's success!

93. As the newest supervisor, I feel like I've been on one of Christopher Columbus's ships for months. I've faced discouragement, fatigue, frustration, and potential mutiny. There have been times I wanted to jump overboard. But finally, I feel as if I've awakened after a

night of terrible storms to see land on the horizon, shining in the bright morning sun. At last I can see that the changes I've made were right.

94. I feel like a Labrador retriever out with some duck hunters who are having a great day! Because I faithfully work hard for them, they shower me with praise and affection. I love this! Shoot some more ducks!

95. I'm like an old baseball glove. Though well-worn, I can still catch. With a helping hand, I can handle anything, even a red-hot grounder!

96. My boss told me that our company used to be like a bucket with a hole two inches from the top. No matter how hard employees worked, they could never fill it with water. But since they added me to the staff, the hole has been patched, and we're doing great. And for the first time in years, the bucket is about to overflow with profit!

97. I'm a mechanic. A few days ago my boss paid me a compliment that made me feel great. He said the work I do around the shop is like the oil in an engine. It makes everything run smoothly with a minimum of friction. Without it, everything would lock up. It's great to work for someone who appreciates me!

98. Our company just gave me a big bonus for landing a huge account. I feel like I'm playing a video game and scoring unbelievably well. The better I do, the more free games I win and the more excited I am about what I'm doing. This is great!

I Feel My Work Can Be Drudgery . . .

99. I feel like a beautiful Arabian racehorse that is only used to give kids pony rides. I constantly walk in a circle. Kids kick me when they get on and off. They drip ice cream on my back. My coat is dusty and matted, and my owner doesn't care one bit. The sun beats down on me. My once-beautiful mane is tan-

gled. My head hangs low in shame. I know that the swift, noble blood of a racehorse is within me. If I only had the chance to be free from this drudgery, then I could show what I'm capable of doing.

100. I feel like a tube of toothpaste. By the end of the day people have squeezed everything they can out of me. My work has really helped the company, and I know I'm appreciated for that. Yet, nobody seems to care that I'm empty and gnarled up inside.

101. The Super Bowl is over and the players file into the locker room. Dirty uniforms are thrown on the floor, along with dirty socks and muddy cleats. The players shower and slowly file out, leaving me behind. Not only do I have to clean up the mess, but no one even knows I'm here doing it.

ENDNOTES

Chapter One

1. While some people may be more familiar with the expression "extended metaphors" or simply "figurative language," we like "word pictures" as a more descriptive term. The expression "word pictures" is found in articles like Carol Huber's "The Logical Art of Writing Word Pictures," *IEEE Transactions on Professional Communication*, March 1985, 27–28.

Chapter Two

1. For a disturbing look at the damage caused by an angry father, see William S. Appleton's insightful book, *Fathers and Daughters* (New York: Berkeley Books, 1981).

2. "When people use a figure of speech today, it is often met with the cry, 'oh, that is figurative'—implying that its meaning is weakened, or that it has quite a different meaning, or that it has no meaning at all! But the very opposite is the case. For a figure is never used except to add force to the truth conveyed, emphasis to the statement of it, and depth to the

meaning of it." E. W. Bullinger, *Figures of Speech* (Grand Rapids: Baker Book House, 1968), 5–6.

Chapter Three

1. *Hunting Licenses and Federal Deer Stamp Sales as Reported by the Information Bureau of the Department of Interior July 15, 1941 through 1942* (Washington, D.C. U.S. Fish and Wildlife Bureau, Federal Aid Office, 1942). Such a furor was caused by *Bambi*'s release that two major outdoor magazines of the day devoted full editorial articles to the issue. To see the movie's negative effect on the deer hunting industry, see Donald C. Pettie, "The Nature of Things," *Audubon Magazine,* September 1942, 266–71. For a pro-hunting viewpoint, see *"Outdoor Life* Condemns Walt Disney's Film *Bambi* as Insult to American Sportsmen," *Outdoor Life,* September 1942, 17.

2. Cicero, *De oratore,* Trans. H. Ranckham, The Loeb Classical Library, 1942 (Cambridge: Harvard University Press, 1977).

3. Cicero, *De inventione,* Trans. H. M. Hubbell, The Loeb Classical Library, 1949 (Cambridge: Harvard University Press, 1976).

4. Aristotle, *"Art" of Rhetoric,* Trans. J. H. Freese, The Loeb Classical Library, 1926 (Cambridge: Harvard University Press, 1975). ˙

5. Charles Lewis, *The Autobiography of Benjamin Franklin* (New York: Collin Books, 1962).

6. When Lincoln first met Harriet Beecher Stowe, he is reported to have said, "So this is the little lady who wrote the book that made this big war!" James Ford Rhodes, *History of the United States,* vol. I (1893); *Lectures on the American Civil War* (1913).

7. Winston S. Churchill, *The Unrelenting Struggle*

(Boston: Little, Brown and Company, 1942), 95. For other examples of the many ways Churchill used word pictures, see Charles Eade (ed.), *Winston Churchill's Secret Session Speeches* (New York: Simon and Schuster, 1946) or *The End of the Beginning: War Speeches by the Right Honorable Winston S. Churchill* (Cassell and Company, 1943).

8. See Chapter Sixteen, "The Dark Side of Emotional Word Pictures."

9. John F. Kennedy, "Inaugural Address," *New York Times*, January 21, 1961, 8.

10. Dr. Martin Luther King, Jr., *Letter from a Birmingham Jail & I Have a Dream* (Atlanta: The Southern Christian Leadership Conference, 1963).

11. Alfred A. Balitzer (ed.), *A Time for Choosing: The Speeches of Ronald Reagan, 1961–82* (Chicago: Regnery Gateway, 1983). Also see T. Marganthau, "Reagan Leaves the Democrats Mumbling," *Newsweek*, October 27, 1986, 29–30, or P. McGrath, "Never Underestimate Him!" *Newsweek*, April 19, 1982, 28–29.

12. S. L. Greenslade, *The Cambridge History of the Bible* (Cambridge: Cambridge University Press, 1973), 479. "The Bible has been read by more people and published in more languages than any other book."

13. John P. Eaton, *Titanic: Triumph and Tragedy* (New York: W. W. Norton & Co., 1986).

14. James and William Belote, *Typhoon of Steel: The Battle for Okinawa* (New York: Harper and Row, 1970), and Commander Herbert L. Bergsma, *Chaplains with Marines in Vietnam 1962–71* (Washington, D.C.: History and Museum's Division, Headquarters Marine Corp, 1985).

15. "Men of the Year," *Time*, January 3, 1969. Astronauts Frank Borman, Jim Lovell, and Bill

Anders read Genesis 1:1–10 on Christmas Eve, 1968, during the mission of Apollo 8.

16. For the parable of the good Samaritan, see Luke 10:29-37. For the reference to many mansions, see John 14:1-3. For the reference to faith like a mustard seed, see Matthew 17:20. And the story of the prodigal son is in Luke 15:11-32.

17. These word pictures are found, in order, in Isaiah 9:6; John 1:1; John 8:12; John 15:5; Revelation 5:5; and Revelation 22:16. God the Father is pictured as one who defends the righteous with a protective shield, Psalm 5:11-12; a rock, Psalm 28:1; a bird who spreads His protective wings over His own, Psalm 91:4; and a refuge and shield, Psalm 119:114.

18. Robert Hoffman, "Recent Research on Figurative Language," *Annals of the New York Academy of Sciences,* December 1984, 137–66.

19. Leonard Zunin. *Contact: The First Four Minutes* (New York: Ballantine Books, 1975).

20. L. D. Groninger, "Physiological Function of Images in the Encoding-Retrieval Process, *Journal of Experimental Psychology: Learning, Memory, and Cognition,* July 1985, 353–58.

21. G. R. Potts, "Storing and Retrieving Information about Spatial Images," *Psychological Review,* vol. 75 (1978): 550–60, and Z. W. Pylyshyn, "What the Mind's Eye Tells the Mind's Brain: A Critique of Mental Images, *Psychological Bulletin,* vol. 80, n. 6 (1973): 1–24.

22. Ibid., Pylyshyn, 22.

23. Among other studies, see A. Mehrablan, "The Silent Messages We Send," *Journal of Communication,* July 1982.

24. Louie S. Karpress and Ming Singer, "Communicative Competence," *Psychology Reports,* vol. 59 (1986): 1299–1306.

25. For an excellent resource on how to deal with differences in a marriage, we highly recommend Chuck and Barb Snyder's *Incompatibility: Grounds for a Great Marriage* (Phoenix: Questar Publishers, Inc., 1988).

Chapter Four

1. S. F. Witelson, "Sex and the Single Hemisphere: Specialization of the Right Hemisphere for Spatial Processing," *Science*, 193: 425–27, and Milton Diamond, "Human Sexual Development: Biological Foundations for Social Development," *Human Sexuality* (Baltimore: Johns Hopkins Press, 1981).

2. J. E. Bogen, "Cerebral Commissurotomy in Man: Minor Hemisphere Dominance for Certain Visuospatial Functions," *Journal of Neurosurgery*, 1965, 135–62, and John Levy, "A Model for the Genetics of Handedness," *Genetics*, 72: 117–28.

3. E. Zaidel, "Auditory Language Comprehension in the Right Hemisphere: A Comparison with Child Language," *Language Acquisition and Language Breakdown* (Baltimore: Johns Hopkins Press, 1978).

4. D. Kimura, "Early Motor Functions of the Left and Right Hemisphere," *Brain*, 97: 337–50.

5. Robert Kohn, "Patterns of Hemispheric Specialization in Pre-Schoolers," *Neuropsychologia*, vol. 12: 505–12.

6. J. Levy, "The Adaptive Advantages of Cerebral Asymmetry and Communication," *Annals of the New York Academy of Sciences*, vol. 229: 264–72.

7. See Chapter Sixteen, "The Dark Side of Emotional Word Pictures."

Chapter Five

1. For the actual biblical account of this riveting word picture, see 2 Samuel 11–12.

2. 1 Samuel 16:1–12.

3. 1 Samuel 17; 2 Samuel 3:1; 5:1–25.

4. Noted Old Testament scholars Keil and Delitzsch comment on David's state of affairs, "These words went to David's heart, and removed the ban of hardening which pressed upon it. There is no excuse, no searching for a loophole, no pretext put forward, no human weakness pleaded. He acknowledges his guilt openly, candidly, and without prevarication." C. F. Keil and F. Delitzsch, *Commentary on the Old Testament in Ten Volumes: Vol. II: Joshua, Judges, Ruth, 1 and 2 Samuel* (Grand Rapids: William B. Eerdmans Publishing, 1975), 391.

Chapter Six

1. Francis Brown, S. R. Driver and Charles A. Briggs, *A Hebrew and English Lexicon of the Old Testament* (Oxford: Clarendon Press, reprinted edition, 1974), "aph," 60, and *The Compact Edition of the Oxford English Dictionary* (New York: Oxford University Press, 1971), "anger," 82.

2. Ibid., Brown, "kilyah," 480, and Oxford, "fear," 973.

3. 2 Samuel 12:1ff.

4. Gary Smalley and John Trent, Ph.D., *The Blessing* (Nashville: Thomas Nelson Publishers, 1986), 172–73.

5. For example, Christ used word pictures with certain groups of people who "had ears but would not hear, and eyes but would not see," Matthew 13:14ff.

Chapter Seven

1. If you've just opened the book to this story, you'll need to go back to portions of chapters 5 and 6, which provide seven steps to creating emotional word pictures, for the steps Jim followed.

Chapter Eight

1. Richard F. Newcomb, *Iwo Jima* (New York: Holt, Rinehart & Winston, 1965), 35.

2. Ibid., 229.

Chapter Ten

1. Wilder Penfield, *The Mystery of the Mind* (Princeton: Princeton University Press, 1984), 148.

2. For a family vacation with a purpose, why not write to one of our favorite places for further information on their outstanding family retreats: Forest Home Conference Center, General Delivery, Forest Falls, CA 92339 or call 714-794-1127.

3. The Performax Personal Profile System (Performax Systems International, Minneapolis, Minnesota).

4. For information on the author's availability, write: Today's Family, Post Office Box 22111, Phoenix, AZ 85028.

Chapter Eleven

1. Gary Smalley, *If Only He Knew* and *For Better or for Best* (Grand Rapids: Zondervan Publishing, 1979); Gary Smalley and John Trent, Ph.D., *The Blessing* and *The Gift of Honor* (Nashville: Thomas Nelson Publishers, 1986 and 1987); Gary Smalley, *The Key to Your Child's Heart* (Waco, Texas: Word Books, 1984).

2. See Jim's word picture in Chapter Seven, "The Well of Nature," and Susan's in the following chapter, "The Well of Everyday Objects."

3. *The Compact Edition of the Oxford English Dictionary* (New York: Oxford University Press), 485.

Chapter Twelve

1. Song of Songs 4:1ff.

2. Song of Songs 2:1ff.

3. William Shakespeare, *Romeo and Juliet,* Act II, Scene I (Oxford: Clarendon Press, 1986), 388.

4. Ibid., 388.

5. Ibid., 396.

6. Elizabeth Barrett Browning, "Sonnets from the Portuguese."

7. Christopher Ricks, *The Force of Poetry* (Oxford: Cambridge University Press, 1984), and J. R. Jackson, *Poetry and the Romantics* (London: Rouledge & Kegan Paul Ltd., 1980).

8. UCLA Monthly, *Alumni Association News,* March–April, 1981, 1.

9. For a challenging look at the origin and creation of affairs, see Willard F. Harley, *His Needs/Her Needs* (Old Tappan, New Jersey: Fleming H. Revell Company, 1986).

10. Marc H. Hollender, "The Wish to Be Held," *Archives of General Psychiatry,* vol. 22 (1970): 445.

11. S. R. Arbetter, "Body Language: Your Body's Silent Movie," *Current Health,* February 1987, 11–13.

12. See our definition of a word picture in Chapter Two, "Words That Penetrate the Heart."

13. Psalm 128:1,3, NIV.

14. See Gary Smalley, *Joy That Lasts* (Grand Rapids: Zondervan Publishers, 1985). In this book, Gary talks of the importance of a dynamic spiritual life as the key to success in all we do. While *The Language of Love* speaks primarily of how word pictures can be used as an effective communication tool, we look forward to doing a book that addresses the incredible power of word pictures to enhance a person's spiritual life.

Chapter Thirteen

1. James C. Dobson, *Dare to Discipline* (Wheaton: Tyndale Publishers, 1970); *Hide or Seek* (Old Tappan, New Jersey: Fleming H. Revell, Power Books, 1974); *Love Must Be Tough* (Waco, Texas: Word Publishers, 1983); Paul D. Meier, *Christian Child-Rearing and Personality Development* (Grand Rapids: Baker Book House, 1977); Richard Allen, *Common Sense Discipline* (Ft. Worth: Worthy Publishers, 1986).

2. James C. Dobson, *Parenting Isn't for Cowards* (Waco, Texas: Word Publishers, 1988).

Chapter Fourteen

1. Gary Smalley and John Trent, Ph.D., *The Blessing,* (Nashville: Thomas Nelson Publishers, 1986).

2. Robert Pandia, "Psychosocial Correlates of Alcohol and Drug Use," *Journal of Studies on Alcohol,* vol. 44, no. 6 (1983): 950; Mark Warren, "Family Background and Substance Abuse," *Psychiatric Research Review,* vol. 35 (1985): 25; Joanna Norell, "Parent-Adolescent Interaction: Influences on Depression and Mood Cycles," *Dissertation Abstracts International,* vol. 45, no. 4-A (1984): 1067; Frank Minirth, Paul Meier, Bill Brewer et al., *The Workaholic and His Family* (Grand Rapids: Baker, 1981); Frank Minirth and Paul Meier, *Happiness Is a Choice* (Grand Rapids: Baker, 1978).

3. Brian Lucas, "Identity Status, Parent-Adolescent Relationships, and Participation in Marginal Religious Groups," *Dissertation Abstracts International,* vol. 43, no. 12-B (1984): 4131; J. R. Heiman, "A Psychophysiological Exploration of Sexual Arousal Patterns in Females and Males," *Psychophysiology,* vol. 14, no. 3 (1987): 2266–74; J. V. Mitchell, "Goal-Setting Behavior as a Function of Self-Acceptance, Over- and Under-Achievement and Related Personal-

ity Variables," *Journal of Educational Psychology*, vol. 50 (1970): 93–104.

4. V. Cosi, *Amyotrophic Lateral Sclerosis* (New York: Plenum Press, 1987).

5. E. M. Goldberg, *Family Influences and Psychosomatic Illness* (London: Tovistock Publishers Ltd., 1987).

6. See Chapter Six, "Creating an Effective Word Picture, Part Two."

7. Cathy Dent, "Facilitating Children's Recall of Figurative Language in Text Using Films of Natural Objects and Events," *Human Development*, July–August 1986, 231–35; Robert Verbrugge, "The Role of Metaphor in Our Perception of Language," unpublished speech presented at the Linguistics Section of the New York Academy of Sciences on January 14, 1980.

8. Deena Bernstein, "Figurative Language: Assessment Strategies and Implications for Intervention," *Folia Phoniat*, vol. 39 (1987): 130.

9. Proverbs 22:6.

10. For an excellent description of what training a child involves, see Charles R. Swindoll, *You and Your Child* (Nashville: Thomas Nelson Publishers, 1977).

11. Proverbs 6:6.

12. S. J. Samuels, "Effects of Pictures on Learning to Read, Comprehension and Attitudes Toward Learning," *Review of Educational Research*, vol. 40 (1980): 397.

13. William Looft, "Modification of Life Concepts in Children and Adults," *Developmental Psychology*, vol. 1 (1969): 445.

14. Gary Smalley, *The Key to Your Child's Heart* (Waco, Texas: Word Publishing, 1984).

Chapter Fifteen

1. Psalm 103:19.
2. Isaiah 55:8.
3. Psalm 23:1-2
4. Psalm 23:4.
5. Psalm 51:11.
6. Romans 3:12-13.
7. Romans 12:1.
8. Isaiah 53:7.
9. Isaiah 53:6.
10. Psalm 3:1, 3.
11. Psalm 18:1-2.
12. Psalm 1:1-3.
13. See Luke 18:1-8 and 11:5-13.
14. Isaiah 40:21, 23-24.
15. John 14:2.
16. Don Richardson, *Peace Child* (Glendale, Cal.: Gospel Light, 1974).

Chapter Sixteen

1. Proverbs 18:21, RSV.
2. Theodore Abel, *Why Hitler Came into Power* (New York: Prentice Hall, 1948).
3. Norman H. Baynes, *The Speeches of Adolf Hitler, Vol. I and II* (New York: Howard Fertig Publishers, 1969). This speech was given in the Kroll Opera House in Berlin on March 23, 1933.
4. Philip Kerns, *People's Temple/People's Tomb* (Plainfield, New Jersey: Logos International, 1979).
5. Edwin Meuller, *Making Sense of the Jonestown Suicides* (New York: Cassel Publishing, 1981).
6. Vincent Bugliosi, *Helter Skelter* (New York: Bantam Books, 1975).
7. Walter Martin, *Kingdom of the Cults* (Minneapolis: Bethany House Publishers, 1985), and a book by a former satanic priest, Mike Warnke, *Satan Seller* (Plainfield, New Jersey: Bridge Publishing, 1987).

8. For a chilling picture of people addicted to verbally inflicting pain on others, see M. Scott Peck, *People of the Lie* (New York: Simon & Schuster, 1983).

9. C. S. Lewis, *The Lion, the Witch and the Wardrobe* (New York: Macmillan Publishing Co., 1950), 75–76.